Series / Number 01-041

Political Institutionalization: Comparative Analyses of African Party Systems

MARY B. WELFLING
Virginia Polytechnic Institute and State University

SAGE PUBLICATIONS / Beverly Hills / London

Copyright © 1973 by Sage Publications, Inc.

Printed in the United States of America

All rights reserved. No part of this book may be reproduced or utilized in any form or by any means, electronic or mechanical, including photocopying, recording, or by any information storage and retrieval system, without permission in writing from the publisher.

For information address:

SAGE PUBLICATIONS, INC.
275 South Beverly Drive
Beverly Hills, California 90212

SAGE PUBLICATIONS, INC.
St George's House / 44 Hatton Garden
London EC1N 8ER

International Standard Book Number 0-8039-0271-9

Library of Congress Catalog Card No. L.C. 73-84898

FIRST PRINTING

When citing a professional paper, please use the proper form. Remember to cite the correct Sage Professional Paper series title and include the paper number. One of the two following formats can be adapted (depending on the style manual used):

(1) NAMENWIRTH, J. Z. and LASSWELL, H. D. (1970) "The Changing Language of American Values." Sage Professional Paper in Comparative Politics, 1, 01-001. Beverly Hills and London: Sage Pubns.

OR

(2) Namenwirth, J. Zvi and Lasswell, Harold D. 1970. *The Changing Language of American Values.* Sage Professional Paper in Comparative Politics, vol. 1, no. 01-001. Beverly Hills and London: Sage Publications.

CONTENTS

I. The Study of Institutionalization 5
II. The Concept of Institutionalization 10
III. Measuring the Institutionalization of African Party Systems 14
    The Sample and Unit of Analysis 14
    Indicators of Institutionalization 18
IV. Scoring and Indexing Party System Institutionalization 27
V. The Level of Institutionalization: 1945-1970 32
    A Construct Validation 37
VI. The Process of Institutionalization: Time Series Analysis 39
    Internal Structure of the Time Series 39
    Trend 40
VII. Discontinuities of Political Independence 45
    Level of Institutionalization: Pre- and Postindependence 46
    Processes of Institutionalization in the Postindependence Period 52
VIII. Institutionalization: Theoretical Relationships 54
Notes 58
References 60

Political Institutionalization: Comparative Analyses of African Party Systems

MARY B. WELFLING
Virginia Polytechnic Institute and State University

Social science literature contains numerous discussions of the concept of institutionalization, but contemporary comparative political science has begun to focus on the concept only over the past decade. This recent literature exhibits little agreement as to what institutionalization actually is, how it can best be measured, or even its theoretical utility. Following a discussion of some of its previous usages, this paper aims to provide a precise conceptualization of institutionalization, develop indicators of that concept, and report on the application of these measures to the study of 31 black African party systems.

THE STUDY OF INSTITUTIONALIZATION

Concern wtih institutionalization is far from a recent development; the study of institutions and processes of institutional change, for instance, has roots in eighteenth- and nineteenth-century sociological thought (Eisenstadt, 1965), and Max Weber's work, at the turn of the century, marks a milestone in the study of social institutions. Weber's concern with institutionalization relates to his attempt to account for the emergence of Western civilization and the legal rational system of modern institutions. In his political sociology,[1] Weber proposed his well-known pure types of domination and their corresponding principles of legitimacy—the charis-

---

AUTHOR'S NOTE: *I want to thank Raymond Duvall for assistance on this monograph, and Kenneth Janda and Jorge Dominguez for comments on an earlier draft.*

matic, traditional, and legal-rational systems. For Weber, institutionalization is the process of building the legal-rational system of institutions. In spite of his structural and typological approach, however, he "flirted with... the underlying psychological and interactional dynamics" (Buckley, 1967: 131), for he observed that men are not only guided in their behavior by norms, but also behave in reaction to each other. Norms associated with the types of domination may guide individual behavior, but at the same time men act in concert with each other on the basis of their interests (Bendix, 1962: 285-290). Institution-building involves the capacity to crystallize norms (i.e., legal-rational ones), but creativity and freedom are found in the process, and there is a continuous tension between the constrictive and creative aspects of institutions (Eisenstadt, 1968: xvii). In other words, the individual does not passively accept and work within the norms of a given institutional setting, but actively may attempt to transform them or preserve them on the basis of his own interests. For Weber, then, institutionalization involves both individual level processes of establishing norms and system level processes of structural definition.

Talcott Parsons represents the next major contribution in sociological discussions of institutionalization, but to him it represents not so much institution-building as an attribute of a system. Unlike Weber who suggested psychological bases of institutionalization, Parsons developed a fundamental dissatisfaction with an individualistic approach and instead turned his attention wholly to interaction and social systems. This new orientation became evident in Parsons (1949), and came to the fore in Parsons (1951a, 1951b). Parsons distinguishes three related systems—culture, social, and personality—and it is the social system that he focuses upon, although it must always be understood in relation to the other two. Culture becomes internalized in the personality and institutionalized in the social system. To Parsons, "a social system is a normative entity based upon the beliefs, values and norms of the membership" (in Mitchell, 1967: 52). When members of the system interact, patterns of reciprocity emerge and these become "role expectations" and "patterns of evaluation." As standards guiding interaction are internalized so as to be significant to the actor and elicit response from others, the standard becomes institutionalized in the social system. In Parsons' (1951b: 20) own words, institutionalization is

> the integration of the expectations of the actors in a relevant interactive system of roles with a shared normative pattern of values. The integration is such that each is predisposed to reward the conformity of others with the value pattern and conversely to disapprove and punish deviance. Institutionalization is a matter of degree, not of absolute presence or absence.

Although Parsons' analyses of institutionalization largely apply to the social system as a whole or to the subsystems which become differentiated to perform his well-known functional needs—adaptation, goal attainment, integration, and pattern maintenance—he also has applied the concept to the international system (Parsons, 1961) and to individual organizations (Parsons, 1956).

A major strand of contemporary sociology, however, has returned to the school of thought developed by Weber and analyzes how institutions are built. Many current theorists, largely in the area of organizational behavior, claim that more attention needs to be given to the individual and to the social-psychological aspects of institutionalization. Philip Selznick (1957), in his study of leadership in administration, for instance, recognizes organizational constraints but stresses the fundamental role of individual interaction, and, in fact, suggests that the leader is an agent of institutionalization who offers a guiding hand to an otherwise haphazard process. The major impetus to this renewed focus on the individual has been research concerned with the level of elementary interaction, and particularly exchange theories. James Coleman (1966: 180) has taken the extreme position of refuting the relevance of norms governing social behavior, arguing that the important starting point is "collective actions and rational actors, each with interests and power relative to these actions." Few would take such an extreme position, however, and what many other exchange theorists propose is that norms and institutions are important but their origins can be traced to the interaction of individuals. George Homans (1961), for example, distinguishes between institutional behavior, which conforms to roles, and subinstitutional behavior, the elementary social behavior which is his primary concern. He claims that elementary social behavior involves a direct exchange of rewards between at least two persons, in which actual behavior and not just a norm specifies what behavior ought to be.

Numerous sociologists, particularly those falling in the category of "social interactionists," develop arguments similar to Homans and bring the focus of attention to the individual level of analysis. Herbert Blumer (1962), for one, argues against relying on structural categories such as social system, culture, norms, values, social stratification, and so forth, for they skip over the people who act in society. Organization is important only in that it provides the framework in which individuals act. It does not determine actions but instead is the product of the activity of individuals.

William Goode (1960) echoes a similar theme in developing his theory of role strain. The view of society which pictures individuals conforming to a set of norms fails to account for many empirical situations in which individuals differ in their value commitments, some to the point of rejecting the central values of society. People never receive any general solutions for all role obligations but instead face a variety of role strains which they must solve. The result is a process of role bargaining that organizes an actor's role system, and the end products of this process are institutions. The existing institutions influence role bargaining, but in turn are subject to modification as a result of role bargaining.

Peter Blau begins at the same point as Homans by analyzing how social exchange, or those actions that are contingent on rewarding reactions from others, gives rise to social structures, but he begins to arrive at a synthesis of the two schools and returns to system properties. The purpose of studying face-to-face relations is to further the understanding of social structures that evolve, and Blau (1964: 20) stresses that "although complex social systems have their foundations in simpler ones, they have their own dynamics with emergent properties."

The concept of institutionalization in the sociological literature thus displays considerable diversity ranging from a stress on the normative-structural aspects to a concern with individual behavior which shapes institutions. The latter constitutes a wide selection of works which converge in challenging the normative-structural approach when it ignores individual behavior. While the internalization of cultural norms and their institutionalization at the societal level may guide behavior to some extent, new norms arise from individual interaction and in turn become institutionalized. Much of the sociological conception of institutionalization seems to be taking a middle position recognizing the relevance of both normative constraints and individual innovation (see Buckley, 1967; Eisenstadt, 1965).

Although a concern with institutionalization probably has been implicit in many comparative political science works, explicit treatments of it are quite recent. Much political development literature, for example, has looked upon political development as a process of building viable political institutions with the capacity to handle problems of modernization (e.g., Eisenstadt, 1966, 1964, 1962, 1957; Pye, 1965; Von Vorys, 1965; Weiner, 1967, 1965; Halpern, 1965; Huntington, 1966; Almond and Powell, 1966; Zartman, 1964), but it was not until Samuel P. Huntington's pioneering article (1965) that a contemporary political scientist isolated institutionalization as a concept worthy of special treatment. Since that time a series of works dealing with institutionalization have appeared, but they spend little time grappling with the concept and defining its precise meaning. Most political scientists seem unaware of the extensive treatment of the concept by classical and contemporary sociologists (the work of Yeager [1972] being a notable exception), and generally they merely suggest a series of "dimensions" or "ingredients" of institutionalization and then hasten to "operationalize" them.

Huntington, for instance, argues that the strength of political organizations depends, first, on the scope of their support, or the extent to which they encompass activity in the society, and second on their levels of institutionalization. The process whereby institutions with absorptive and initiative capacity acquire value and stability is defined as institutionalization, and this is the essence of political development (Huntington, 1965: 394). But after Huntington devotes one sentence to defining institutionalization, he spends the remainder of his efforts devising indicators of the concept, suggesting we measure four dimensions—adaptability/rigidity, complexity/simplicity, autonomy/subordination, and coherence/disunity. While his discussions of the four dimensions are sufficient, Huntington never adequately explains why it is these four dimensions that characterize institutionalization.

Most authors follow Huntington's pattern of proposing a series of ingredients of institutionalization. Nelson Polsby (1968) claims an institutionalized organization must be bounded, complex, and characterized by universalistic and automated decision-making, and he proceeds to apply these criteria to the U.S. House of Representatives; Benjamin and Ori (1970), who are interested in party institutionalization in Japan, offer three dimensions of scope, complexity, and autonomy; Robert Keohane (1969) applies the concept to international organizations and looks for differentiation, durability, and autonomy; Ted Gurr (1968: 1105) suggests institutionalization involves "the extent to which societal structures beyond the primary level are broad in scope, command substantial resources and/or personnel, and are stable and persistent," and, though less explicit, Paul Brass (1969) seems to conceive of it involving some degree of organization (complexity) and stability.

There are exceptions to this principle of simply enumerating dimensions, but by and large these exceptions merely view institutionalization as a single dimension. Raymond Hopkins (1970, 1969) focuses, like Parsons, on the formulation of norms which govern patterns of behavior. In his study of Tanzanian elites, he attempts to measure consensus on the roles of administrator, legislator, and president, for to him:

> (a) political system is institutionalized ... when there is a stable set of expectations about how decisions will be made and order maintained such that random shocks or the deviant behavior of a few men cannot alter the basic pattern of political life [Hopkins, 1969: 7].

A similar, but less explicit, normative view appears in Benjamin and Pedeliski's (1969) study of the Minnesota public defender system. Finally, Yeager (1972) takes a very different approach by focusing on institutional stability and change at the micropolitical, or small-group, level, relying heavily on sociological notions of exchange.

It is clear, then, that political scientists have conceptualized institutionalization in numerous ways. Most agree with others on some ingredients of the process but no two arrive at the same final combination of elements. Criticisms of the conceptual and operational approaches of these studies appear elsewhere (Kesselman, 1969; Janda, 1969: 11; La Palombara, 1969; Rustow, 1969; Welfling, 1971: 63-78), but the fundamental problem seen running through all these works is that they tend to pay very little attention to conceptualization; with few exceptions there is no real attempt to explain why particular dimensions are suggested. All of these studies are oriented toward an empirical assessment of institutionalization, but valid empirical analysis needs first a sound conceptual base.

THE CONCEPT OF INSTITUTIONALIZATION

Institutionalization has been handled in essentially one of two ways. First, it has been viewed as a process of building institutions with an emphasis on the role of individual behavior. Second, it has been viewed at the system level either as a combination of elements that characterize a system (e.g., Huntington), or, in a Parsonian orientation, as the crystallization of norms guiding behavior. Although some contributions of social interactionists and exchange theorists are incorporated in the following conceptualization, the systemic perspective is accepted as the more useful orientation. A concern with the role of individual behavior is, perhaps, useful and feasible for the study of small groups or organizations, but for the student of large-scale social systems, interpersonal interactions must, necessarily, be reduced in significance both at the conceptual and measurement levels. On the other hand, the Parsonian framework is also not accepted as a satisfactory approach to institutionalization, for Parsons' emphasis on the crystallization of norms easily leads to the view that institutions are based on shared values and consensus. Recent sociological studies increasingly emphasize that systems can be and often are institutionalized with considerable conflict and strain (Buckley, 1967). Instead, a general systems perspective provides the basis for developing a consistent and acceptable definition of institutionalization. The following conceptualization arrives at an enumeration of four dimensions which define institutionalization, but unlike other works in comparative politics dealing with the concept, these dimensions are deduced from a set of axioms on how social and political systems behave.[2]

The principal definition is that institutionalization is the process of crystallizing (i.e., defining, creating, developing, maintaining) social institutions, and the extent or degree of institutional characteristics at any time. An institution is a social system that is either established or capable of becoming established, that is a social system capable of endurance. The perspective adopted here is largely stimulated by Buckley (1967) and views an open (e.g., social) system as some set of stably interrelated and interdependent variables or processes which in the performance of certain activities and the pursuit of certain goals are bounded in that they can be differentiated from an environment, and which, in goal-seeking behavior, constantly exhibit a degree of tension with an ever-changing environment. Buckley's perspective, then, contains two defining characteristics and one principal axiom. The defining characteristics are (1) that system variables or processes are stably interrelated, and (2) that system processes are bounded or can be differentiated from an environment. The principal axiom is that the system processes are in constant tension with a threatening environment.

A second axiom relates to the establishment of a social system and it is that a system persists to the extent that it can map and/or reduce threatening environmental tensions, a requirement that is met in two ways:

(1) Established systems or institutions in interaction with their environment have some impact or effect on that environment, and can modify it so that it is less threatening and more compatible with system goals.
(2) Through structural elaboration and differentiation (morphogenesis), the system adjusts its internal configuration to better cope with changes in the environment.

The potential for structural elaboration is constrained. The institution is necessarily characterized by structure—stable and regular patterns of interaction among components—and morphostatic processes (e.g., negative feedback) which strive to maintain that structure. So institutions can be characterized neither as manifesting no change nor exhibiting complete freedom to fluctuate at will. Rather, system survival in a threatening environment implies constant change but within a range that is constrained by stable interactions among components (Ashby, 1960). Stability and adaptability are necessary and complementary aspects of any social institution, the recognition of which is congenial to the previously mentioned sociological consensus which recognizes the simultaneity of normative constraints and individual innovation.

It follows directly from the foregoing definitions and axioms that institutionalization involves four essential elements. The first characteristic is *boundary,* such that the system can be differentiated from its environment and that a set of activities specifically internal to the system are distinguishable from activities in the environment. Others have employed the notion of autonomy (Huntington, 1965; Polsby, 1968; Keohane, 1969) but autonomy seems to imply closure in which the system is independent of units in the environment. Boundary, on the other hand, refers to the delineation and definition of the system; boundaries are permeable and permit considerable interaction with and dependence upon the environment.

A second dimension essential to institutionalization is that of patterned behavior or *stability* (the second basis for a definition of system), applying to both intra- and extrasystem interactions. Actors and units within the system manifest patterned sets of behavior vis-à-vis one another and the system as an entity behaves in regular ways in relation to actors in the environment. This dimension, however, does not imply a normative value basis. While some writers such as Parsons and Hopkins have approached institutionalization from a systems perspective, the present position objects to their consensus orientation and admits that systems of interaction can be institutionalized even with considerable conflict and strain. The important point is not the institutionalization of norms—an approach which becomes indistinguishable from legitimacy—but the persistence of patterns of interaction among units (Buckley, 1967).

Third, institutionalization implies some impact on the environment. Established systems affect their environments and increased institutional character means greater capability for environmental impact. Thus extensiveness or *scope* is another dimension. Activities are not only patterned and stable but also of some importance, such that the behaviors and activities of other actors must take account of the existence of the institutionalized system.

A fourth dimension or characteristic essential to institutionalization is that of *adaptability*. System components must be able to adjust to changes occurring within the system as well as to those emanating from the environment in order for the system to endure. Others have suggested persistence or durability as a dimension of institutionalization (Keohane, 1969), but actual persistence is really an ex post facto test of adaptability, for systems which have endured for long periods are likely to have been adaptive. One advantage of focusing on adaptability, rather than actual durability, is that it applies to relatively new organizations and does not require a study of systems that have existed for generations. Huntington's measures, for example, generally call for this long-range perspective.

Complexity is an additional dimension that some authors (Huntington, 1965; Polsby, 1968; Benjamin and Ori, 1970; Brass, 1969) have included as part of institutionalization but it is rejected here as not essential. Systems differ in their complexity, for although all systems are internally differentiated and thus demonstrate some complexity, the degree to which the system becomes differentiated and elaborated depends upon the environments with which it interacts, the tensions and strains to which it must adapt, and the activities in which it must engage. Systems with different levels of complexity could be institutionalized, and thus complexity does not appear to be a defining characteristic of institutionalization.

In sum, institutionalization is a process which occurs as elements continue to interact in some relatively stable pattern, and in their interactions create and elaborate structures and develop boundaries, which distinguish them from their environments. The constraints of structure are not unchanging, however, for they are constantly adjusting as the system adapts to internal and external strains. This system of interacting elements not only develops and elaborates structure (stable patterns of internal behavior) but also regular and predictable interactions with the environment, and it has sufficient scope to have an impact on that environment. Finally, institutionalization is viewed not only as a process, but also as a state, condition, or property of a system at any point in time, a distinction elaborated on more fully in later analyses.

Three points should be made explicit. (1) Institutionalization should not simply be equated with social systemicity or entitivity, a position the author once mistakenly accepted.[3] While institutionalization requires a base in systemicity, it implies more—in particular, the capability of becoming an established social system. (2) A related point is that the dimensions of establishment (i.e., scope and adaptability) are not necessarily implied in the dimensions of systemicity. Our world is filled with examples of short-lived social systems which have not demonstrated an ability to become established. (3) This discussion is not intended to imply a notion of unidirectionality of process. On the contrary, it should reveal the tenuous character of institutionalization for social systems, particularly in terms of a balance between morphogenetic and morphostatic processes. The increasingly common position that many Western political institutions are losing an ability to adapt and adjust implies that the balance required for institutionalization may not be easy to maintain.

MEASURING THE INSTITUTIONALIZATION OF AFRICAN PARTY SYSTEMS

THE SAMPLE AND UNIT OF ANALYSIS

A series of indicators of the four dimensions of institutionalization have been developed in an effort to provide a sufficient base on which to measure the institutionalization of African party systems. Measurement implies two things: first, the indicators must approximate the concept in the abstract, and, second, they must be appropriate in the concrete to the sample employed. The units to which the concept of institutionalization is applied in this research are African party systems. The sample consists of party systems in independent, sub-Sahara Africa, excluding Southern Africa and contemporary colonies. Ethiopia is not part of the sample since it has had no party system, and Swaziland and Equatorial Guinea (Rio Muni) have been omitted because of the recency of their independence. The remaining sample includes 31 countries.[4]

This focus has severe implications for the measurement of institutionalization. The size of the sample means, first, that indicators to be developed must be measurable through secondary research since field research is not feasible, and, as all Africanists are well aware, the sample dictates that we must cope with a dearth of documentation. The following attempts to develop indicators suggest the limitations that poor documentation has placed on this research effort, and it is readily admitted that given a broader data base and more comparable information across countries, opportunities for measurement would have been greatly enhanced, and the validity of the analysis improved.

In spite of these difficulties, however, this sample was selected as particularly relevant for a couple of reasons. On the one hand, literature on African politics has tended to reduce the importance of political parties. In the early 1960s Western scholars saw political parties as perhaps the most important political institutions for newly independent black Africa, but following the rash of military coups in the mid-1960s, they tended to the other extreme and practically denied any relevance to parties at all. Thus, some assessment of the actual role of parties in developing African nations appears in order.

The potential relevance of parties to new African political systems was recognized early by African scholars. The primary function often claimed for political parties in new African nations is their ability to further national integration. This is an argument set forth especially for the single party but more generally for multiparty systems also. While some parties form along tribal lines and, hence, hinder national unity, the party is a modern organization that potentially can recruit from all sectors, cut across social groupings, and provide a nationwide input mechanism. If it contains a well-articulated and effective structure, it can reduce separatist antagonisms (Wallerstein, 1960; Zolberg, 1963; Emerson, 1966). W. A. Lewis (1965) even argues that a party system representing the plural society (i.e., parties along tribal or regional lines) can further unity under proper governmental arrangements such as proportional representation and coalition government, which permit major parties a role in government and, hence, provide them with a stake in the national state.

Other functions attributed to political parties in new nations are that they are the organizations most capable of leading the process of modernization, they provide an ideology helping to maintain adhesion to policy, and they mobilize support and participation. Through control of patronage, they extend their organizations to the local level and thus develop a national communications network and provide a link for the populace to the national government. Finally, parties can help to express and aggregate interests, recruit and train new leaders, and provide a position for opposition (Silvert, 1965; Douglas, 1963; Chambers, 1966).

The positive contributions of political parties began to be questioned, however after several years of independence when it became clear that these supposedly all-powerful organizations were unable to fulfill the functions attributed to them. In many cases they made little contribution to economic development, failed to extend their organization and recruit larger segments of the population, and frequently hindered national integration rather than furthering it. Interparty competition seemed to exacerbate cleavages in cases such as Sierra Leone (SLPP versus APC) and Nigeria (NCNC versus NPC versus AG), while the inability of single parties to equally represent tribal or regional groups created antagonisms in other states.

Upon independence, governing parties depleted their ranks as they had to fill government positions. Government responsibilities preempted the time and energies of party officials, and government agencies rather than party meetings came to make important decisions. Thus the party became less active and in many cases participation declined. It has been argued that the party tends to take over government, but in Africa it appeared that the government was taking over the party, and instead of the emergence of one-party systems, one found the creation of no-party states (Wallerstein, 1966; Bienen, 1971; Rotberg, 1966).

Even students of African parties who early emphasized their strength and importance, reassessed their significance and changed their original position. Aristide Zolberg (1964), for example, once stressed the positive functions of political parties, especially in the Ivory Coast, but later revised his original position and questioned the impact of parties:

> An examination of political parties, the best studied feature of the African scene, reveals such a wide gap between the organizational model from which the leaders derived their inspiration and their capacity to implement such schemes, that the very use by observers of the word "party" to characterize such structures involves a dangerous reification [Zolberg, 1968b: 72].

The sudden rash of military coups and the removal of political parties from the governing scene confirmed these new appraisals of parties and led African political observers to focus their interests on military governments and to consider political parties a thing of the past.

It is clear that the original assessments of African parties overstated their importance or at least failed to predict their lesser role in the independence period. But to ignore their study leaves many questions unanswered and forgets that parties may yet have a role to play. If it is assumed that the African populace will in time become increasingly participant, some mechanisms are necessary to organize this participation. Samuel Huntington, for one, argues strongly that the major institutional device for such organization is the political party or party system. He also argues that the earlier a society develops well-organized parties, the better able it will be to handle expanding participation. The stronger the political parties, the more stable will be the political system. He argues that the party is a stabilizing influence not only in Western societies, but the experience of modernizing countries such as Mexico and Turkey indicates that it is a relevant device in the non-Western setting as well. Moreover, many countries ruled by the military have found it expedient to create new parties to organize participation (Huntington, 1968: ch. 7; see also Miller, 1970: 548). One finds this pattern already developing in Africa in situations such as Zaire, where Mobutu formed his ruling Mouvement Populaire Revolutionaire (MPR), and Congo (Brazzaville) with the establishment of Ngouabi's Labor Party (PCT).

Henry Bienen, a student of Tanzanian politics, has also admitted the weakness of political parties even in a seemingly strong party system such as Tanzania. But he does not deny the continuing relevance parties may have:

> the remaining ruling single parties have real roles to perform. Neither military forces nor civil services are likely to make up in performance and effectiveness what they lack in legitimacy and political know-how. Public order and political participation, which are

preconditions for economic development and are the essence of political development, are not going to be guaranteed by the removal of parties [Bienen, 1970: 82].

Though not the omnipotent organizations once perceived, African political parties may not be the irrelevant reification of Western observers that others suggest. Even granting some political parties a lesser significance, one can still accept that others may have been or may be relevant political actors. If parties have fulfilled the functions attributed to them by many scholars, however, they must have acquired a certain strength and stability or, as Huntington suggests, a certain level of institutionalization. Thus the perspective of institutionalization is a useful one by which to examine the role of African political parties, and, more important, party systems.

In approaching the institutionalization of parties in the African context, it becomes necessary to make the distinction between individual parties and party systems, for while individual organizations may be institutionalized, their operation in a party system may not be. The distinction between the two levels is rarely made, and this omission has led in part to the confusion over assessments of parties in Africa. It is not a sufficient condition that individual parties become institutionalized, for they must also function in the established context of a party system. It is this latter aspect that has proven to be the difficult condition to achieve and has raised doubts about the durability and impact of parties in Africa (Welfling, 1971: 101-105). As William Chambers (1966: 94) argues, the role of parties depends on the party system:

> The ultimate impact parties have depends on the party system. Whether there is one party or more than one makes a difference; the kinds of relationships that exist between parties where more than one appears also count; and so does the kind of leadership that develops within the parties.

Another argument for focusing on the party system as unit of analysis is more theoretical. A later discussion will mention the theoretical utility of institutionalization, especially as it relates to the question of political instability. Although political institutionalization can refer to a variety of political subsystems, party system institutionalization is of particular theoretical importance, since the party system has been defined as that system which most directly links the public with the government. One would expect mobilized populations to engage in various forms of strife in the absence of institutionalized links between publics and governments. This significance of the party system is certainly not new.

Putnam (1967) has found an empirical relationship between stability of the party system (employing Banks and Textor data) and the propensity to military interventions in Latin America; Michael Taylor and V. M. Herman (1971) demonstrate that characteristics of the party system are of consequence for government stability, using measures such as length of governments as an indicator; and Huntington (1968: 401, 420) argues,

> In modernizing society "building the State" means in part the creation of an effective bureaucracy, but more importantly, the establishment of an effective party system capable of structuring new groups into politics.... In terms of political development what counts is the strength and adaptability of the party system.

For these reasons, then, the focus of this research is on the institutionalization of party systems in black Africa, and measurements must be appropriate for this particular sample.

INDICATORS OF INSTITUTIONALIZATION

Indicators must be not only appropriate for the sample but they must also approximate the concept of institutionalization in the abstract. All indicators are imperfect approximations of a concept and the following suggestions are no exception. Campbell (1969: 15), for instance, stresses the error component in any indicator and argues that an appropriate manner in which to minimize error in concept scores is to utilize multiple operationism:

> we have only *other invalid measures* against which to validate our tests; we have no "criterion" to check them against. A theory of the interaction of two theoretical parameters must be tested by imperfect approximations of each.... In this predicament, great inferential strength is added when each theoretical parameter is exemplified in two or more ways, each mode being as independent as possible of the other.... This general program can be designated *multiple operationism*.

While the present research is not strictly an example of multiple operationism in that different and independent measurement strategies are not employed, something of the logic of multiple operationism is employed in the form of multiple indicators. Because all of the following indicators are assumed to be in part errorful (but errorful in unrelated ways), the extent to which indicators overlap provides a less errorful approximation of the concept.[5]

Boundary

The insitutionalization of a system involves the creation of boundaries and the system's differentiation from its environment. Boundary is defined in part by the incidence of higher interactions and interdependence within the system as opposed to outside the system. Poor documentation or limitations of secondary research prevent the use of many feasible indicators such as the ratio of within-system to outside-system interactions (Deutsch, 1963), the channeling of career opportunities (Polsby, 1968; Keohane, 1969), and boundary ambiguity as determined by the degree of overlap with other subsystems in performing system activities.

It would be most useful to assess the degree or extent of boundary between the party system and the government or executive branch, especially given the suggestion that African party systems are becoming increasingly indistinct from the government, but feasible indicators are very difficult to suggest. On the other hand, one can document the activity of nonparty personnel in the party system and the extent to which they participate in it. When individuals run in elections and attempt to link constituents to the government (i.e., the primary party system goal) without identifying with components of the party system, boundaries tend to be ambiguous. Thus, the percentage of seats held by independents is used as an indicator for boundary—the larger the percent, the less differentiated are boundaries. The percentage of seats won by independents is recorded for each election year, and nonelection years are treated as missing data.[6] Although several countries have had no independents, we find 23% of the seats going to independents in the 1962 election in Sierra Leone and 20% in the 1957 election in Dahomey.

Stable Patterns of Interaction

An institutionalized party system exhibits stable patterns of interaction. This dimension includes both intrasystem interactions, or those occurring among entities of the system, and extrasystem interactions, or those relating the system to other relevant systems, particularly the public and government. This dimension is unusually difficult to tap, for the essence of patterned interactions is that units operate on the expected behavior of others, a situation difficult to assess through secondary research.

In terms of extrasystem behaviors, an institutionalized party system exhibits stable links with other relevant systems, especially the public and government. While the creation of expected channels for recruitment and filling positions of authority is conceptually important, feasible indicators are difficult to suggest. On the other hand, stable interactions between the public and party system are equally important and somewhat easier to measure. The links between the party system and public are many, involving levels of support for parties, patterns of support (e.g., ethnic or religious), patterns of recruitment, and so forth, but documentation enables calculation of only the levels of party support. Assessing changing levels of support for the components of the system is different from measuring level of public support for or involvement in the party system. This latter aspect, or level of participation, is included later in scope. The former aspect involves stability of intrasystem interactions, for if component units are fluctuating in relative strength, patterned behavior among those units is more difficult.

"Legislative Instability" is used to indicate the stability of interactions between the public and component parties. This variable is scored by summing the yearly changes in the percentage of seats held for each party.[7] For example, consider a system with three parties. In 1958 each held 33% of the seats, and in 1959 one (A) held 67%, one (B) held 33%, and one (C) held none. The yearly percentage change from 1958 to 1959 would be calculated as follows:

Party	1958	1959	% Change
A	33	67	34
B	33	33	00
C	33	00	33
Total Change 1958-1959:			67

Three countries—Ivory Coast, Liberia, and Malawi—record no instability since their ruling parties have held 100% of the seats throughout the time period. On the other hand, Burundi has a mean yearly change score of 62% and Dahomey 60%.

Intrasystem interactions involve two aspects of importance. The first aspect relates to the set of entities in the system, for the more the set of entities changes, the more unstable the interactions will be. It is easier for one entity to operate on the expected behavior of the others when those entities are fairly constant, rather than changing. Of primary interest are the reshuffling of existing entities and the entrance and exit of entities to and from the system.

"Splits," "mergers," and "name changes"[8] are three alternative ways of modifying or changing the set of existing entities in a party system, and "new entities" refers to the creation or dissolution of parties to or from the system. Splits, mergers, and name changes are scored after the founding of the first party (or 1945 if founded before that) and new entities after the creation of a party system. Each score is calculated yearly by weighting the occurrence of an event by the importance of the parties involved, where importance is measured as the proportion of legislative seats held by the party,[9] since it is assumed that the larger the party, the more impact it has on the system's institutionalization. A mean score is taken for the proportion of seats won by the splitting entity in the two elections (or equivalent time points) following the split to determine the importance of the new party to the system. When one or more minor parties join a major one, the combined legislative strength of the merging parties constitutes the score of the merger. The score is calculated as the mean percentage of seats won at the two elections previous to the merger. When two or more fairly equal parties merge, however, and create a new entity in which none of the original parties clearly predominates, the merger is weighted by the legislative strength of the new party and the score calculated as the mean percentage of seats won at the two elections following the merger. Name changes have received a weight according to the mean proportion of seats previous to the name change.[10] Finally, the score for each new entity is based on the mean proportion of legislative seats won at the two elections following its founding or at the two elections previous to its leaving the system.

Again, some countries experience none, or few, of these events of instability. Burundi, however, receives the highest score on splits primarily because of a series of splits from UPRONA in 1961; Dahomey's highest score on mergers is especially due to the joining of the RDD, PRD, and MLN to form the PDU in 1960, and the UDD and PND to form the PDD in 1964; Zaire emerges the extreme case on new entities since hundreds of small parties arose between 1958 and 1964; and Dahomey and Zaire experience the most name changes in the total time period, six and five respectively.

Another aspect of intrasystem interactions is the set of behaviors in which the entities engage. When interactions are stable, behavior will be fairly constant, but when the forms of interaction change and the behaviors of the entities alter, it becomes difficult to operate on the expected behavior of others. "New forms of interaction" is concerned with the creation and dissolution of coalitions and alliances, or changing between behaviors of cooperation and competition. The scoring of this indicator not only considers the legislative strength of parties but also the proportion of the parties in the system that are involved. Scores of each event are calculated as: combined legislative strength multiplied by proportion of the parties involved. Sudan and Togo have the highest mean yearly scores on this variable. Sudan's score is explained by the creation and dissolution of the Umma and Ashiqqua coalition in 1946 and the various alliances among Umma, NUP, and PDP in 1956 and 1958. Togo's score, on the other hand, results from the CUT and JUVENTO coalition (1958) and dissolution (1960) and the alliance of all major parties (PUT, JUVENTO, MPT, and UDPT) in 1963.

Scope

The third dimension essential to institutionalization is scope. This dimension means that an institutionalized system has an impact of some significance on its environments; that is, its activities are of importance to other actors and systems such that the latter must take into account the presence of the former. The scope of the party system vis-à-vis the government is conceptually important but again feasible indicators are difficult to create for the African context. Scope in terms of the public, however, is easier to assess through secondary research, if scope is meant to reflect the impact the party system has on segments of the public that desire to make inputs to the government. Scope implies both a vertical and horizontal aspect.[11] First, a system broad in scope would extend beyond the elite and affect the mass public, and levels of "electoral participation" are taken to be indicative of this aspect. Each election year is scored as the percentage of the population voting, with scores carried over to subsequent elections. Participation rates exhibit considerable variation. Only 3% of the population voted in Malawi's 1964 election, while Gabon claims 56% voted in 1964 and Ivory Coast boasts over 40% voting in all four elections since 1959.

Horizontal scope, on the other hand, relates to a system's impact on a wide range of social and geographical sectors. Although patterns of ethnic support or penetration are relevant here, available election results provide a clue only to geographical scope, or "national orientation," and in addition permit scoring only at one point in time—the independence election. Scoring of this variable is based with some modifications, on a scale of national orientation developed by Janda (1970) to score individual parties. Originally the attempt was made to score every party, but documentation for party systems is so variable that to make scores across systems comparable, only those parties with legislative representation were scored. The scale runs from two to six, that is from a totally regional to a totally national party. The score for national orientation of the party system is the mean score of all parties winning legislative seats in the independence election. Several countries scored "6," that is nationally oriented (e.g., Ivory Coast, Liberia, Tanzania), but Ghana and Nigeria scored 3.0 and Zaire lowest at 2.20.

Adaptability

The fourth dimension of institutionalization involves the system's ability to persist through its adaptability. This dimension is similar to the second, stable patterns of interaction, in that it involves both an intrasystem and an extrasystem aspect. An institutionalized party system demonstrates the ability to adjust to both internal and external strains—unless a party system can accommodate existing parties or adapt to new articulative interests, it will be unable to persist and function effectively as a system and hence become institutionalized.

Adaptability, then, is an attribute of the party system indicated by the behavior of units in the system. It is somewhat easier to take a negative approach and to suggest indicators of unadaptive behavior, assuming that the absence of these indicators means the party system is adaptive. Included in a set of unadaptive behaviors, first, are attempts to hamper opposition party activity. "Electoral discrimination" (generally employed by a ruling party against competitors) could take the form of postponing elections, invalidating elections, or requiring that all parties present candidates on a single list for the entire country as a single constituency. Since none of these three variables alone provides sufficient variation, the three are combined into a single indicator of electoral discrimination. They are scored only for the postindependence years, since the colonial government determined the electoral system previously. These variables are scored yearly as either 0 or 1—0 meaning an election was not postponed (or invalidated or single list used), and 1 meaning that an election was postponed (or invalidated or single list used). Eight countries have experienced no electoral discrimination from independence through 1970 (or the end of the party system)—Botswana, Burundi, Liberia, Nigeria, Somali Republic, Sudan, Tanzania, and Zambia—but, scoring highest on the composite variable, Uganda postponed an election (due in 1966) for five of its eight independent years, Ghana postponed the 1961 election until 1965 and then employed the single list, and Dahomey used the single list in all of her postindependence elections.

A second indicator of adaptability is "legal single party." When a party is declared the only legal one, other parties are prevented from arising. The more years that a party is the only legal one, the less adaptable the system is. This variable is scored yearly as 0 or 1 to indicate whether or not there was a legal single party. Legal single party, like electoral discrimination, can be scored only for the postindependence years. Fully 19 African countries had not yet been declared legal single parties by the end of 1970, but Chad was a legal single-party state for eight of her first ten years of independence and Malawi for five of her first six independent years.

Four additional indicators of adaptability represent behaviors which destroy entities or prevent their creation. "Arrests," "partial bans," "bans," and "refusing registration" as events reflect unadaptive system responses. As they have been scored, they reflect not only this unadaptive character but also scope (in weighting for success of the action) and boundary (in weighting for size of party acted against). They have been scored in a similar manner which takes into consideration the size of the party acted against and the success of the action, for the more successful the action, the more the party system is capable of structural definition, and indeed is capable of influencing its environment, hence, is characterized by adaptability and scope. Scoring of these variables begins with the granting of internal self-rule, when ruling African parties obtained the power to legally restrict the activity of other parties.

Since so many entities acted against are new parties that have never had an opportunity to hold legislative seats, using the exact proportion of legislative seats held as a weight for party strength would require too many estimates. The method employed instead simply involves identifying a party's potential or actual strength as minor (one with no legislative representation), moderate (one with 10% of the seats or less), or major (one with more than 10% of the seats).

Success of action also consists of three categories—(1) complete success, (2) partial success, and (3) no success. Judging the success of an action requires knowledge of its effects on the party acted against. If the action was completely successful, the party, in the case of a ban, would have been effectively destroyed, or, in the case of arrests or partial bans, hindered such that later actions would be unnecessary. Partial success entails weakening the party acted against but not causing its complete destruction. If a ban or arrest reduces the legislative representation of a party but the party continues to provide active opposition, then the action would be regarded as partially successful. No success occurs when the action fails to affect the object party which continues equally strong and active.

Table 1 depicts the matrix developed for scoring arrests and bans. The first factor, success of action, is weighted more heavily since success is taken to be primarily indicative of the system's scope and ability to adapt—the less successful a party is in banning potential components (or arresting leaders), the less able it is to define its own structure and to modify its environment. The size of the party acted against has also received some weight—the larger the party, the higher the score (i.e., less institutionalized). One could argue that the score should be higher, the smaller the party, since a system unable to cope with the existence of a fairly insignificant party could not be considered adaptive. On the other hand, size, or significance, of party appears more indicative of the boundary dimension than adaptability per se. If a system (or its components) is attempting to restrict emergent units from that system, there is ambiguity as to what that system contains. The larger and more important is the party restricted from the system, the more ambiguous are the boundaries of that system. Thus, the matrix in Table 1 provides a measure not only of adaptability (success in defining system components and structure), but also to a lesser extent of scope and boundary (significance of potential components excluded). Each event receives a score from the matrix and yearly scores are obtained by summing all events in a year (0 if no event). Since partial bans and refusing registration exhibit little variation across the sample, they have been aggregated with bans (partial bans being weighted half as much as a ban) to create a single variable representing attempts to limit opposition entities.

Botswana, Gambia, and Sudan show no recorded arrests between internal self-rule and 1970 (or the end of the party system), but Togo, which scores highest on this variable, exhibits unsuccessful arrests of major party leaders from 1961 through 1966. Lesotho ranks next to Togo with unsuccessful and partially successful arrests of leaders of major (BCP) and moderate (MFP) parties from 1966 through 1970. Eight countries show no bans, including partial bans and refusing registration. In contrast, Zaire witnessed one partial ban (ALCO in Leopoldville) and three unsuccessful or partially successful bans of moderate parties (PSA-Gizenga, DAU, and MPA) before the end of her party system in 1965, and Burundi

TABLE 1
SCORING MATRIX FOR ARRESTS, BANS, PARTIAL BANS, REFUSING REGISTRATION[a]

Party Size (b)		Success (a)		
		Complete 1	Partial 3	None 5
Minor	1	4	10	16
Moderate	2	5	11	17
Major	3	6	12	18

a. Formally, the cell entry and, hence, score for an event is given as $x = 3a + b$.

experienced unsuccessful bans of three moderate parties (UPP, PDC, and MPB) before her military coup of 1966.

Validity of the Indicators

The previous section has not only presented the 13 indicators of institutionalization but also has stressed the difficulties encountered in developing valid indicators of a complex concept in the African context through secondary research. The resulting set of indicators is not offered as perfect measures but instead as the best feasible ones given the limitations of documentation.

In spite of subsequent tests for convergence and theoretical construct utility, the possibility remains that the indicators do reflect some phenomenon other than party system institutionalization. One possibility suggested is that the indicators in fact reflect governmental control over electoral and parliamentary processes, and that African parties in becoming indistinct from government organizations are thus actually more uninstitutionalized. However, indicators reflecting government control (bans, arrests, electoral discrimination) do indeed give countries lower party system institutionalization scores. Since indicators with no base in government control are included and do covary with measures of government control, the only logical conclusion is that government control of the party system is part of the uninstitutional character of that system. In short, it is not a distinct concept but at most a contributory component.

A second and possibly more troublesome suggestion is that the indicators are tapping primarily stability.[12] If this is the case it would imply that, in the language of the previous conceptual discussion, the indicators are tapping systemicity rather than the established or institutional character of the system. In some respects that argument has some real plausibility. It may be that the indicators measure whether what are called party systems are indeed political systems, and in addition it may be that relative to a worldwide sample viewing African party systems as institutions is inappropriate. The best response to that position seems to be that several of the indicators do reflect scope and adaptability (i.e., ability to become established) and in the sense the measurement is of institutionalization rather than simply systemicity.

SCORING AND INDEXING
PARTY SYSTEM INSTITUTIONALIZATION

The thirteen indicators of institutionalization—percent independents, legislative instability, splits, mergers, name changes, new entities, new forms of interaction, arrests, bans, electoral discrimination, legal single party, electoral participation, and national orientation—were scored for the period 1945-1970 for those years in which at least one political party existed.[13]

Institutionalization is taken here, however, as a system characteristic and as such can only be applied to some set (greater than one) of interacting and interdependent entities. For an emerging party system, the process of institutionalization would require the existence of two or more parties. Lacking a more precise measure of "entitivity" the first date of simultaneous existence of two or more parties is taken to mark the emergence of a potential party system. As that system acquires some level of "systemicity" or concreteness, parties can drop out without a loss of potential systemness, so long as remaining parties (or a single party) contain differentiable components that interact, are interdependent, and function to link publics with governments. It is with the elimination of all parties or the prohibition of parties from government activity that the system is taken to become extinct. Events such as bans or arrests that result from a military coup which ends the party system are not coded since interest centers only on activities of the party system itself and since institutionalization scores are later used to predict military coups. Coding of such events would build in unwarranted relationships. Party systems which have revived after military governments have been coded but are not included in later analyses of institutionalization. Table 2 gives the relevant dates for the coding of all indicators for each party system.

While it is necessary for the researcher to enumerate a set of indicators that are conceptually adequate and appropriate to the universe of study, generating an index of institutionalization requires that one assess the extent to which the indicators represent a single unidimensional concept. This question is essentially one of interitem reliability or internal validity—the degree to which the indicators converge on the central concept of institutionalization. Correlational and factor analysis are conventional techniques employed to assess concept unidimensionality. If a concept is conceived as a single dimension, those variables supposedly indicating that concept must share a major portion of their variation in common.

Since one would not necessarily expect yearly covariation among the

TABLE 2
RELEVANT YEARS FOR PARTY SYSTEM CODING[a]

Country	First Party[b]	Party System Established[b]	Party System Ended	Self-rule	Independence
Botswana	1959	1962	not yet	1965	1966
Burundi	1957	1959	1966	1961	1962
Cameroun[c]	1948	1949	not yet	1957	1960
CAR	c1946	c1946	1966	1957	1960
Chad	1945	1946	not yet	1957	1960
Congo (br.)	1946	1946	1963	1957	1960
Dahomey	1946	1946	1965	1957	1960
Gabon	1946	1948	not yet	1957	1960
Gambia	1951	1951	not yet	1964	1965
Ghana	1947	1949	1966	1951	1957
Guinea	1946	1955	not yet	1957	1958
Ivory Coast	1946	1946	not yet	1957	1960
Kenya	1959	1959	not yet	1962	1963
Lesotho	1952	1957	1970	c1965	1966
Liberia	1945	1945	not yet	(1839)	(1847)
Malawi	1945	1958	not yet	c1964	1964
Mali	1945	1946	1968	1957	1960
Mauritania	1946	1948	not yet	1957	1960
Niger	1946	1948	not yet	1957	1960
Nigeria	1945	1949	1966	1954	1960
Rwanda	1957	1957	1973	1962	1962
Senegal	1945	1946	not yet	1957	1960
Sierra Leone	1949	1950	1967	1960	1961
Somali	1945	1946	1969	1956	1960
Sudan	1945	1945	1958	1954	1956
Tanzania	1954	1956	not yet	1961	1961
Togo	1946	1946	1967	1958	1960
Uganda	1945[d]	1955	1971	1962	1962
Upper Volta	1945	1948	1966	1957	1960
Zaire	1950	1957	1965	none	1960
Zambia	1948	1958	not yet	1964	1964

a. A detailed explanation of all coding and a listing of all coded events appears in Welfling (1971: App. A).

b. If before 1945, 1945 is recorded since that is the beginning of the time period of analysis.

c. Dates apply to East Cameroun. For an explanation of the procedure used to aggregate scores for East and West Cameroun see Welfling (1971: 281-285).

d. For purposes of analysis events are scored beginning in 1952 with the founding of the UNC, rather than with the Bataka Party which was banned for several years.

indicators, convergence over a longer time period is a fair test. For that reason, mean yearly scores for the entire time period 1945-1970 are employed to determine unidimensionality. An examination of the correlation matrix of these summary indicator scores standardized by number of years of party system existence, reproduced in Table 3, demonstrates that electoral discrimination, legal single party, and electoral participation exhibit consistently poor relationships with the other variables and with each other. Because of the low correlations it is of little conceptual utility to include these three indicators in a principal components analysis. Their exclusion results in a correlation matrix of 45 cells, 33 (or 73%) of which exhibit correlations above .35, suggesting that the remaining 10 variables do share a considerable portion of their variation in common.

Table 4 reproduces the structure of the first principal component resulting from a factor analysis of the 10 indicators. The results of the principal components analysis demonstrate that the 10 indicators do indeed represent a single underlying dimension. The loadings of the variables range from .51 to .89, and more than half the total variation in the set of 10 can be explained by a single index of that underlying concept. The factor loadings indicate that stable patterns of interaction, particularly as represented by legislative instability and new entities, and adaptability, as represented by bans, are critical aspects of the single concept of institutionalization. Scope of the party system as indicated by national orientation also interrelates highly with those two aspects. The notion of boundary seems to be the least empirically important but that is probably due to a dependence on a single and highly imperfect indicator. The results are certainly sufficiently attractive to generate confidence that the scores produced for each of the cases do represent relative levels of party system institutionalization.

Although a principal components analysis provides an acceptable indexing technique for the summary indicators of institutionalization, it entails two major problems—it is very difficult to generate factor scores with missing data and the procedure is conceptually sensible only if indicators all intercorrelate. Missing data pose a considerably greater difficulty in yearly analyses than for the summary period 1945-1970 since aggregated scores for the twenty-five-year period eliminate the problem of missing data. And, secondly, principal components analysis would be problematic with the inclusion of several variables—electoral discrimination, legal single party, and electoral participation—because they did not intercorrelate with the others.

An alternative is to employ a simple linear additive model across all indicators. The most conventional method is to transform variables to standard score form and calculate the mean standard score across all indicators as the concept score (Janda, 1971). In addition this mean standard score technique enables the calculation of standard deviations of the standard scores for each case, an option not possible with factor

TABLE 3
CORRELATION MATRIX OF THIRTEEN INDICATORS

Variable	1	2	3	4	5	6	7	8	9	10	11	12	13
1. Percentage independents	1.												
2. Legislative instability	.35	1.											
3. Splits	.38	.62	1.										
4. Mergers	.36	.60	.41	1.									
5. New entities	.29	.61	.38	.17	1.								
6. Name changes	.10	.53	.32	.48	.55	1.							
7. New interactions	.31	.52	.10	.23	.50	.21	1.						
8. Electoral discrimination	.03	.04	.04	.09	−.18	−.10	.05	1.					
9. Arrests	.36	.60	.41	.22	.50	.25	.41	.21	1.				
10. Bans	.33	.81	.72	.30	.75	.45	.36	.03	.69	1.			
11. Single party	.11	−.16	−.29	.05	−.30	−.02	−.07	.29	−.12	−.17	1.		
12. Electoral Participation	.28	−.08	−.32	−.10	−.39	−.19	−.21	.42	−.06	−.28	.04	1.	
13. National orientation	.36	−.57	−.36	−.45	−.64	−.55	−.61	.05	−.53	−.45	.27	.19	1.

TABLE 4
FIRST PRINCIPAL COMPONENT FOR TEN INDICATORS OF INSTITUTIONALIZATION

Variable	Factor Loadings
Percentage independents	.51
Legislative instability	.89
Splits	.67
Mergers	.57
New entities	.79
Name changes	.63
New interactions	.60
Arrests	.71
Bans	.86
National orientation	−.78
Percentage variance explained	51

scoring techniques. The primary advantages of the technique are that it can handle missing data, it makes no necessary assumptions about correlations among variables, and by reporting standard deviations, it provides an indication of indicator convergence for each case.

A comparison was made between factor scores and mean standard scores to determine how much distortion the technique introduces over the factor analytic, best-fit solution. Table 5 lists the rankings of the 31 party systems according to three different indexing procedures. The correlation between factor scores using the ten indicators in Table 4 and mean standard scores using these same ten is almost perfect (.99), indicating that the latter method is an excellent approximation of the former. Employing all thirteen indicators also provides a nice relationship with both the factor scores and the mean standard scores of ten indicators (both .97). In other words, inclusion of the three adaptability indicators not included in the principal components analysis introduces less than 6% error, assuming that the factor scores represent perfect measurements. Recognizing that their inclusion could introduce error into the concept score, they do remain conceptually important. In addition, their poor intercorrelations likely are due not only to a lack of true convergence, but also to the different time period on which they are based (postindependence years only), and to the brevity of this time period which has not yet permitted consistent patterns to emerge.

The largest differences among scores appear in the group of highly institutionalized party systems (though not exclusively), but even though absolute scores differ somewhat, the same six systems still appear among the seven most institutionalized ones. Using the thirteen indicators makes

Malawi, Mali, and Dahomey less institutionalized, while Liberia, Gabon, and Somali become more institutionalized. Liberia, however, retains the same rank as the most institutionalized party system, and Dahomey retains the same rank as second most uninstitutionalized.

It is clear that the inclusion of electoral discrimination and legal single party affects these shifts, for Malawi, Mali, and Dahomey all became legal single parties fairly early, and Mali and Dahomey have employed the single list. Liberia, Gabon, and Somali, on the other hand, have not employed the single list, and only Gabon became a legal single party (though fairly late in the time period). Participation has also affected the shifts, for Malawi had an unusually low rate of participation (primarily because the party has been uncontested), while Gabon has reported unusually (in fact at times unfeasibly) high participation rates.

One effect of including these three indicators is suggested by the standard deviations reported in Table 5. A small standard deviation means that a party system scores fairly consistently across indicators, while a large one indicates that a party system scores high on some and low on others. Since the three variables did not relate well with the others one would expect that their inclusion would decrease the consistency of scores across variables for each party system. Inspection of the standard deviations reveals that this is indeed the case, for in all but seven cases they increase considerably when thirteen rather than ten indicators are employed (note the extreme jump for Malawi). But while inclusion of the three variables reduces internal scoring consistency, it is conceptually important. This latter point is exemplified by the countries that experience scoring changes, where the score from thirteen indicators seems intuitively more appropriate. Thus, omission of the three would seem to overestimate the institutionalization of some party systems (e.g., Mali and Malawi) while apparently underestimating others (e.g., Gabon).

In sum, the relationships among the three scaling techniques are sufficiently strong to warrant the use of mean standard scores across all thirteen indicators for the indexing of institutionalization in later analyses, thus permitting the inclusion of conceptually important variables and easing the problems introduced by missing data.

THE LEVEL OF INSTITUTIONALIZATION: 1945-1970

The institutionalization scores based on 13 indicators, which are reported in Table 5, are the basis for an analysis of the condition (or level) of institutionalization of African party systems for the overall period

TABLE 5
PARTY SYSTEM INSTITUTIONALIZATION SCORES—
THREE ALTERNATIVE TECHNIQUES

A: Factor Scores (10 indicators)		B: Mean Standard Scores (10 indicators)			C: Mean Standard Scores[a] (13 indicators)		
Country	Score[b]	Country	Score[b]	St. Dev.	Country	Score[b]	St. Dev.
1. Zaire	1.298	Zaire	2.02	1.14	Zaire	1.57	1.41
2. Dahomey	.889	Dahomey	1.49	1.05	Dahomey	1.35	1.08
3. Burundi	.649	Burundi	1.05	1.20	Burundi	.66	1.28
4. Togo	.558	Togo	.87	.94	Sierra Leone	.62	.92
5. Sierra Leone	.376	Sierra Leone	.71	.96	Togo	.61	.96
6. Upper Volta	.368	Upper Volta	.53	.96	Ghana	.57	.78
7. Ghana	.328	Ghana	.51	.76	Upper Volta	.40	.94
8. Sudan	.205	Sudan	.38	.84	Uganda	.30	.58
9. Lesotho	.198	Lesotho	.36	.91	Sudan	.27	.98
10. Uganda	.192	Uganda	.30	.55	Lesotho	.21	.94
11. Kenya	.130	Kenya	.29	.99	Kenya	.15	.98
12. Nigeria	.064	Nigeria	.14	.74	Chad	.12	.82
13. Congo, B.	.033	Cameroun	.08	.74	Congo, B.	.07	.69
14. Cameroun	.030	Congo, B.	−.00	.73	Nigeria	.05	.84
15. Somali	.010	Somali	−.03	.55	Cameroun	−.07	.72
16. Chad	−.039	Zambia	−.04	.73	CAR	−.09	.80
17. Zambia	−.127	Chad	−.21	.71	Somali	−.20	.60
18. CAR	−.148	CAR	−.22	.83	Guinea	−.27	.89
19. Niger	−.194	Gambia	−.27	.70	Mali	−.28	.88
20. Gambia	−.197	Niger	−.35	.33	Zambia	−.29	.70
21. Rwanda	−.253	Rwanda	−.43	.38	Niger	−.30	.48
22. Gabon	−.259	Gabon	−.44	.43	Gambia	−.37	.64
23. Senegal	−.313	Senegal	−.50	.62	Senegal	−.37	.68
24. Guinea	−.357	Guinea	−.53	.41	Rwanda	−.40	.55
25. Botswana	−.387	Mali	−.63	.40	Malawi	−.45	1.02
26. Mali	−.399	Botswana	−.63	.37	Mauritania	−.48	.74
27. Mauritania	−.473	Mauritania	−.76	.36	Gabon	−.54	.65
28. Tanzania	−.523	Tanzania	−.84	.23	Botswana	−.55	.58
29. Malawi	−.543	Malawi	−.87	.28	Tanzania	−.56	.78
30. Ivory Coast	−.557	Ivory Coast	−.90	.19	Ivory Coast	−.77	.54
31. Liberia	−.560	Liberia	−.91	.18	Liberia	−.91	.20
	$r_{AB} = .99$		$r_{AC} = .97$			$r_{BC} = .97$	

a. Boxed data indicate extant systems; all others have experienced a coup and been replaced by a military regime. See discussion on p. 37.

b. Negative signs indicate relative institutionalization, positive signs indicate relative uninstitutionalization.

1945-1970. The scores range from 1.57 for Zaire to −.91 for Liberia, producing a considerable range of variation. Figure 1 is a presentation of the distribution of institutionalization scores. Examination of the histogram in that figure indicates that there are a couple of extreme cases at both ends of the scale. Liberia and Ivory Coast are highly institutionalized, while Zaire and Dahomey are highly uninstitutionalized. The remaining 27 systems, however, tend to cluster around the center, though with a clear cleavage existing between those that are relatively institutionalized and those relatively uninstitutionalized.

The standard deviations of the standard scores around their means reveal an interesting feature of the institutionalization scores. The standard deviations (also reproduced in Table 5) show a fairly clear relationship with the scores—the higher the score, the higher the standard deviation. In other words, highly institutionalized party systems (i.e., low scores) seem to be consistently institutionalized. On the other hand, uninstitutionalized party systems (i.e., high scores) seem to be less consistent across indicators with high scores on some variables but low scores on others. Examination of the scores of each individual indicator, however, did not reveal any pattern in terms of certain variables scoring high and others low for all or most of the uninstitutionalized systems. That is, two systems that are equally uninstitutionalized can be uninstitutionalized in different ways and for different reasons. Figure 2 depicts a hypothetical relationship between the scores and standard deviations approximating that just described.

Of particular significance is the fact that the institutionalization rankings do not appear to depend on any obvious factor, or simple explanation. This is not to imply that institutionalization has no causes, but that common differentiators among African countries do not correspond with levels of institutionalization. The question of causes is handled more fully elsewhere (Duvall and Welfling, 1973) and mentioned briefly later in this paper. Whether a system is high or low on institutionalization does not seem to depend on colonial regime, recency

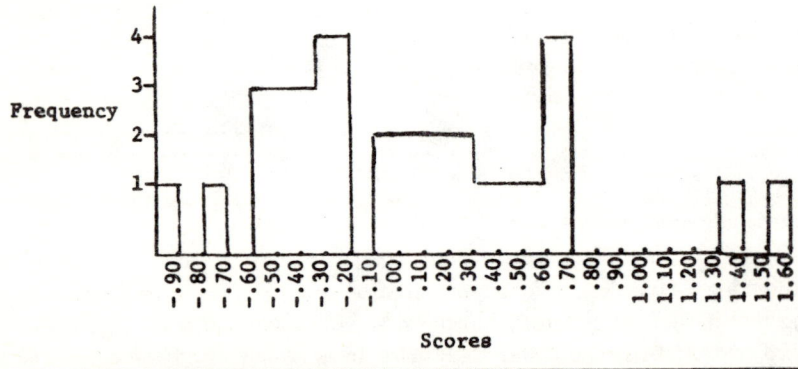

Figure 1: DISTRIBUTION OF INSTITUTIONALIZATION SCORES

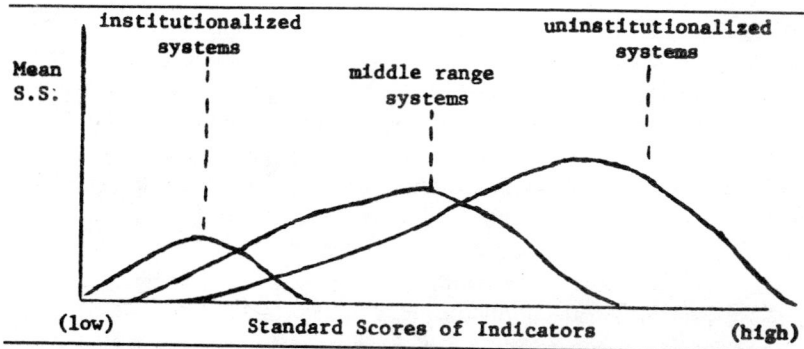

Figure 2: THE RELATIONSHIP BETWEEN MEAN STANDARD SCORES AND THEIR STANDARD DEVIATIONS ACROSS INDICATORS

of independence, or length of experience with party activity. Belgium, for instance, provided indigenous parties the least opportunity to function effectively in the political system. As might be expected, Zaire and Burundi are highly uninstitutionalized, but at the same time Rwanda is the eighth most institutionalized system. France had relatively consistent policies across her colonies, but Dahomey and Upper Volta exhibit low levels of institutionalization while Ivory Coast and Mauritania exhibit high levels. English colonies also distribute themselves along the institutionalization scale, with Sierra Leone and Ghana at the lower end and Botswana and Malawi at the higher. Large differences also appear among those territories that were under UN mandate. These territories were administered with the explicit goal of self-rule (which could be conjectured to be conducive to institutionalization). But again Tanzania appears third most institutionalized while Togo is fifth most uninstitutionalized.

Another factor which might explain party system institutionalization in the period 1945-1970 is the time of independence. Liberia, independent in 1847, is the most institutionalized. However, Sudan and Ghana, the next two of the sample to obtain independence, are relatively uninstitutionalized. Party systems with the same year of independence exhibit highly different levels. Dahomey and Ivory Coast, both independent in 1960, rank thirtieth and second (from most institutionalized), while Lesotho and Botswana, both independent in 1966, rank twenty-second and fourth, respectively.

Length of experience with party activity also does not correspond with levels of institutionalization. Although Liberia has over 100 years of party experience and is the most institutionalized, Dahomey, Togo, Ivory Coast, and Mauritania—extreme cases at both ends of the scale—all had parties in the 1940s. On the other hand, Zaire, Burundi, Rwanda, Lesotho, and Botswana, in which party activity did not develop until later in the 1950s, also distribute themselves along the scale of institutionalization. In other words, factors which differentiate party systems in terms of their historical development do little to explain levels of institutionalization.

Nor do institutionalization rankings correspond to other classifications of African party systems. One of the most common differentiators is the single-/multiparty distinction. The institutionalization rankings seem to cut across this classification with some single-party systems appearing highly institutionalized and others highly uninstitutionalized. For instance, Liberia, Ivory Coast, and Tanzania are most institutionalized, but at the uninstitutionalized end of the scale Dahomey, Ghana, and Upper Volta appear. On the other hand, Botswana and Gabon, multiparty systems throughout most of the time period (Gabon became a single-party state in 1968), rank close to the first three single parties, while Zaire and Sierra Leone, two other multiparty systems, have positions closer to Ghana and Upper Volta.

One interesting difference between the institutionalized and uninstitutionalized single parties is suggested by the rankings in Table 5. All of those with low scores are what one could call "natural" one-party states. That is, from the beginning of the party system, there has been one dominant party with practically uncontested support. In Liberia, Ivory Coast, Tanzania, Mauritania, and Malawi a single party arose early and attracted overwhelming support from the population. None of these parties ever experienced a serious challenge from an opposition party, although several weak and ephemeral parties have appeared in all five systems. Dahomey, Upper Volta, and Ghana, in contrast, were multiparty systems before independence, with no party realizing uncontested superiority. In those countries a single party was imposed, with the banning and harassment of opposition parties that retained support among substantial segments of the population. Gross classifications of single-/multiparty systems have obscured these differences, but institutionalization cuts across these classifications nicely and points to interesting differences among party systems that others have categorized as similar.

Another classification that has done much to shape assessments of the nature of African party systems is that of Coleman and Rosberg (1964) which is based on both ideology and structure. They identify the pragmatic-pluralist pattern and the revolutionary-centralizing trend, and isolate Senegal, Ivory Coast, Sierra Leone, and Cameroun as belonging to the first group and Guinea, Mali, and Ghana as belonging to the second. Again the rankings of institutionalization do not correspond to this classification at all. Ivory Coast is highly institutionalized, Senegal somewhat institutionalized, Cameroun is borderline, and Sierra Leone is highly uninstitutionalized. Similarly, Ghana appears uninstitutionalized while Guinea and Mali are only slightly institutionalized.

In conclusion, the concept of institutionalization does create a classification of African party systems that is fundamentally different from previous ones. It in no way parallels distinctions based on number, structure and/or ideology and it presents a ranking of party systems that breaks out of the conventional categories used to differentiate party systems.

A CONSTRUCT VALIDATION

Validity refers to the question: "To what extent is one measuring the concept he thinks he is measuring." Face validity was involved when indicators were developed; that is, when indicators were suggested as representative of the concept of institutionalization. Convergent or internal validity was discussed in a previous part of this paper when the interrelationships among the indicators were investigated. An additional question is that of construct validity, or how the concept of institutionalization relates to other concepts with which it is theoretically linked.

Relationships between institutionalization and forms of political instability will be mentioned later, but the following discussion deals with the relationship between institutionalization and one form of political instability to suggest the validity of the institutionalization scores. Theoretically, institutionalization has been related to elite (as opposed to mass) instability such that low levels of political institutionalization are likely to lead to coups (Zolberg, 1968b; Huntington, 1965). One could argue that when the primary link between publics and government fails to adapt to new demands, other political subsystems (primarily the military which in many African countries has a broad public base) are likely to step in. Similarly, when party system boundaries are ambiguous, and stable party links between publics and government do not develop, nonparty groups (again, generally the military) may well perform that linkage function, and in the end, formally abolish the party system. Thus, one could argue that party systems ranking low on institutionalization (that is high scores) are most likely to have been terminated by coups. Table 5 which ranks party systems on institutionalization indicates those systems which have or have not experienced successful military takeovers. The systems that are circled in Table 5 still exist (1972), and those that are not circled have experienced a coup d'etat and been replaced by a military regime. Lesotho has experienced an illegal seizure of power, though not a military takeover. It should be stressed again that events surrounding a coup are not coded in institutionalization scores so that all scores are temporally prior to a coup, and are in that sense, truly predictive. One sees that the twelve party systems ranking highest on institutionalization are still in existence, while the ten most uninstitutionalized ones (including Lesotho) were abnormally terminated. The middle range countries exhibit a less clear pattern, with five of the nine having had coups. In spite of the ambiguities in this middle zone, however, the pattern strikingly supports the validity of the concept of institutionalization: fourteen of the seventeen (or 82%) party systems with negative scores (i.e., they are relatively institutionalized) are still in existence. The three systems terminated by coups are CAR, Mali, and Somali. Alternatively, twelve of the fourteen (or 86%) party systems with positive scores (i.e., they are, or were, relatively uninstitutionalized) have been terminated by a coup, the two deviants being Chad and Kenya. Based on this analysis one might predict their future termination, although later time series analyses provide additional insights.

In summary, the results of this static analysis of the entire period 1945-1970 have created institutionalization scores for each party system which rank them in a manner that parallels no previous classification. In addition, a brief investigation into a construct validation of the institutionalization rankings suggests that institutionalization not only provides a new perspective on party systems but it also is an important concept in predicting some forms of instability, a point covered more thoroughly later. The results also negate the arguments that there is little meaningful variation among the 31 countries, and that it is not feasible to explain different patterns of political events across them. For instance, Aristide Zolberg (1968a: 72) has argued that nothing has been able to predict African political phenomena (specifically coups) for the variation among the nations is simply too slight. He states:

> The February, 1966, coup in Ghana dealt a serious blow to any attempt at multivariate analysis. What do Mauritania, Senegal, the Gambia, Mali, Guinea, Ivory Coast, Cameroun, Chad, Niger, Gabon, Rwanda, Kenya, Uganda, Tanzania, Zambia, and Malawi have in common, compared to the other newly independent states, except that so far there has been no successful military challenge to the authority of their leaders.[14]

It appears, to the contrary, that the countries in his list do have something in common—they all, with the exception of Chad, Kenya, and Uganda (which has since had a coup), have negative scores on institutionalization; that is they are relatively institutionalized political party systems. In other words, there does seem to be a useful differentiator among

African party systems, and the 1966 coup in Ghana may not have dealt such a serious blow to attempts at multivariate analysis of African politics after all.

THE PROCESS OF INSTITUTIONALIZATION: TIME SERIES ANALYSIS

Institutionalization is defined above as a condition of systems for some period of time and as a process characterizing systems through time. This distinction between condition and process is essentially the distinction that is often made between "being" and "becoming," where condition is taken to mean focus on system state, while process or "becoming" is taken to mean focus on system change (Miller, 1965). Thus far we have examined institutionalization for the state of the party system during the period 1945-1970. In this section we turn to an examination of process and the question of "becoming," which is investigated through time series analysis of party system institutionalization scored yearly. Analysis focuses only on those years in which a potential party system can be thought to have been in existence; that is, years from the first coexistence of two indigenous parties until the end of the party system or until 1970. Time series, or process, analysis involves essentially two features. The first is an examination of the internal structure of the series, such as trend and fluctuations about trend, and the second investigates causes of variations in the time series.

INTERNAL STRUCTURE OF THE TIME SERIES

Institutionalization scores were produced for each year for each country by standardizing variables across all years and all countries and employing the mean standard score technique discussed above. This procedure provides yearly measures for each country relative to all countries. Additionally, scores were produced by standardizing variables across years for each country separately, providing a time series for the country in which each year's score is relative only to other years for that country. This latter method was employed since a country's development or decay relative to its own prior experience could be as relevant as cross-country comparisons. Although reference will be made to the country-specific scores, the following analyses rely primarily on measures scored across all countries since this procedure makes country scores more comparable. In addition, it provides a larger universe on which to base standard scores (thus reducing the significance of extreme or random fluctuations) and also makes the process analysis comparable to the condition analysis which of necessity is based on scores over all countries.

In assessing any process it is imperative to ascertain whether the variables of concern manifest any change over time. For present purposes that implies a determination of variance about the mean yearly level of institutionalization. If there is little variance through time, the party system can only be interpreted as maintaining a given state rather than "becoming" something different, and we would have to conclude that no process of development or decay is occurring. Investigation of the variances of the 31 countries revealed that all party systems, with the possible exception of Liberia (variance about mean level = .003 where scores are in standard score units), manifest sufficient temporal variation to be experiencing a process of becoming more or less institutionalized. To examine process we can investigate two aspects of the time series—first, the regularities of the series, particularly trend (Holtzman, 1963), and second, discontinuities in the series (Campbell, 1963). Trend represents a smooth, regular, continuous movement in a given direction and is analogous to "evolutionary" changes, while discontinuities are abrupt changes or jumps in the level of a series and are analogous to "revolutionary" changes. Both can represent significant processes as exemplified by the rotting of a log and the explosion of an atomic bomb as relatively extreme physical examples.

TREND

Of primary interest for understanding regularities is the question of trend which is a general rise or fall in mean level. Thus, a trend in party system institutionalization would indicate a systematic rise or fall in the level of institutionalization over time. Three measures are employed here to assess the nature of trend in each of the time series. The first measure relies on linear least-squares regression utilizing each year as an observation and calculates the equation for a line of best fit according to the classical least-squares regression criteria. The slope of the linear least-squares regression of insitutionalization on years serves as a measure of trend. Second, the slope is significant in terms of ability of trend to account for variation in the series. The measure employed is an F-statistic which tests the hypothesis that the trend is significantly different from zero. Third is the question of sequential dependence, or the extent to which the level at one year depends on previous years. Sequential dependence is measured by an autocorrelation coefficient which indicates the relationship between observations at various points in time. A strong positive autocorrelation coefficient indicates that observations are sequentially dependent, and hence that the value of institutionalization is largely dependent on immediately prior years.

These three measures of trend—slope, significance of slope, and autocorrelation—should converge to demonstrate whether or not a party system is experiencing a general and systematic rise or fall in level of institutionalization. Thus a system with a strong and significant slope (either positive or negative) and a high positive autocorrelation (set at .30 for present purposes) would be concluded to be exhibiting a real trend in institutionalization.

Table 6 presents the three trend measures for the 31 party systems measured over all countries and suggests that at least seven systems have been, or were, experiencing a trend in institutionalization. Dahomey, Chad, Mauritania, Tanzania, Mali, Ivory Coast, and Kenya all have significant slopes and autocorrelations above .30. Although Ivory Coast does have a statistically significant negative (i.e., institutionalizing) slope and autocorrelation, the slight magnitude of that slope would suggest that were it a real trend it would be virtually insignificant as a process. A detailed examination of the separate indicators of institutionalization for each year reveals that there is no basis for concluding that a real and institutionalizing trend is occurring. Indeed the one variable on which Ivory Coast obtains a relatively uninstitutional score is electoral discrimination which occurs relatively late in the postindependence period. That this does not effect an uninstitutionalizing trend is due to the greater number of indicators included for the postindependence period on which Ivory Coast is scored as highly institutionalized. An average over the greater number of indicators is more than able to compensate for the uninstitutional scores on electoral discrimination. Of the remaining six countries with clear trends all but Kenya have been moving in an uninstitutionalizing direction (positive slopes).

Three countries in Table 6—Malawi, Liberia, and Niger—exhibit strong autocorrelations but their slopes are not significantly different from zero. Using country-specific scores, however, both Malawi and Niger do demonstrate significant slopes (Malawi has a slope of $-.49$, Niger of $-.024$), indicating that they too might be experiencing a real trend. Liberia's strong autocorrelation, on the other hand, is almost certainly due to its lack of temporal variance mentioned above; if a system is maintaining a given level with little fluctuation about that level, each observation would appear dependent on previous ones.

In general the trend measures for the party systems measured in a country-specific way corroborate the results shown in Table 6. The major exception to this rule is Tanzania which exhibits an uninstitutionalizing

TABLE 6
MEASURES OF TREND—SCORED OVER ALL COUNTRIES[a]

Country	Slope	F	Autocorrelation
1. Zaire	+.090	0.431	
2. Dahomey	+.067	6.317	.32
3. Congo, Br	+.029	2.070	
4. Togo	+.029	1.786	
5. Ghana	+.023	1.840	
6. Chad	+.016	4.948	.45
7. Mauritania	+.013	13.517	.70
8. Tanzania	+.012	5.890	.39
9. Mali	+.010	2.002	.63
10. Sierra Leone	+.010	0.068	
11. Lesotho	+.006	0.055	
12. Malawi	+.004	0.055	.32
13. Guinea	+.003	0.054	
14. Liberia	−.001	0.363	.53
15. Ivory Coast	−.004	5.173	.62
16. Somali	−.005	0.232	
17. Cameroun	−.008	0.331	
18. Upper Volta	−.010	0.120	
19. CAR	−.011	0.245	
20. Gabon	−.011	2.459	
21. Gambia	−.011	0.472	
22. Sudan	−.012	0.110	
23. Senegal	−.013	1.070	
24. Niger	−.014	1.420	.35
25. Nigeria	−.016	1.126	
26. Rwanda	−.017	0.831	
27. Burundi	−.018	0.026	
28. Zambia	−.025	0.727	
29. Botswana	−.046	1.810	
30. Uganda	−.047	1.698	
31. Kenya	−.100	5.773	.66

a. Positive signs indicate a movement in an uninstitutionalizing direction, negative signs an institutionalizing direction. In general F-statistics of 8 or above are significant at the .01 level, of 4 or above at the .05 level, of 3 at the .10 level, of 2 at the .20 level, and of 1.5 at .25 level. All autocorrelations are at lag one except for Kenya which is at lag three.

trend relative to all countries (+.012, F = 5.89) and an institutionalizing trend relative only to itself (−.034, F = 3.796). In Tanzania most events indicative of an uninstitutional system occurred in the early years and thus in relation only to its own past trend is institutionalizing but in relation to other countries these early events were relatively slight and had little effect on the scores for these years. On the other hand, the fact that Tanzania became a legal single party has little effect on within country trend since that condition existed for some period of time, but in relation to other countries the creation of a legal single party is sufficiently extraordinary to strongly affect scores and hence produce a trend of uninstitutionalization. Although a scoring discrepancy such as this is uncommon, it demonstrates the utility of supplementing scores over all countries with country-specific scores. In Tanzania's case the country-specific score (i.e., slope is institutionalizing) is probably more valid since with a few exceptions uninstitutional events occurred early in time and the single fact that Tanzania became a one-party state does not warrant an uninstitutionalizing slope.

This analysis of trend suggests that the majority of party systems have probably not experienced a general and systematic rise or fall in mean level of institutionalization, at least for the total period 1945-1970. Measures of trend converge to demonstrate that Dahomey, Chad, Mauritania and Mali experienced or are experiencing a decline in level of institutionalization, while only Kenya is experiencing a rise. By supplementing scores over all countries with scores by country, it appears that Tanzania is probably experiencing an institutionalizing trend, and though borderline cases, Malawi and Niger also probably have experienced a general rise in the level of institutionalization.

The fact that only a minority (8 of 31) of our party systems has experienced a significant trend during the overall time period, however, does not negate the relevance of process, or "becoming." On the one hand, the reason for relatively few trends could be that the period 1945-1970 is not the appropriate period for analysis, and if we were to take a different time slice, either longer or shorter, we might obtain somewhat different results. On the other hand, it is still possible to demonstrate the importance of process as we have measured it for the sample during 1945-1970. The previous analysis of condition or level reported a construct validation in which institutionalization was used to discriminate those countries which had or had not experienced successful military coups. The results were that condition or level could discriminate the two groups with the exception of some middle-range countries (approximately five misclassifications resulted). If process, or what the system is becoming, is as important as overall level of institutionalization, knowledge of a system's trend should help to account for the deviants found in that analysis.

Figure 3 locates each party system[15] according to its overall level of institutionalization (1945–1970) and its slope for the same time period. If both level and process are important in predicting the occurrence or nonoccurrence of coups one should be able to locate a line in the two-dimensional space such that all coup countries fall above the line and all noncoup countries below the line. The line drawn in Figure 3 is nearly such a perfect discriminator in that it successfully separates the two groups with only two exceptions—Chad and Cameroun—thus improving our ability to discriminate coup and noncoup countries over knowledge of level alone.[16]

Several important observations should be made explicit. First, previously misclassified systems—most notably, Kenya and Mali—can be readily accounted for when their strong and significant trends are considered. Second, our ability to discriminate with only two deviants remains even if all countries of insignificant trend (using an F of 2.0 as a cutting point for significance) are treated as if their slope is zero (i.e., placed on the X-axis). In fact, such an assumption of zero slope increases the range of possible locations of the true discriminant function, as shown in Figure 3 by the dashed line, such that any equation between $Y = -.23X - .058$ and

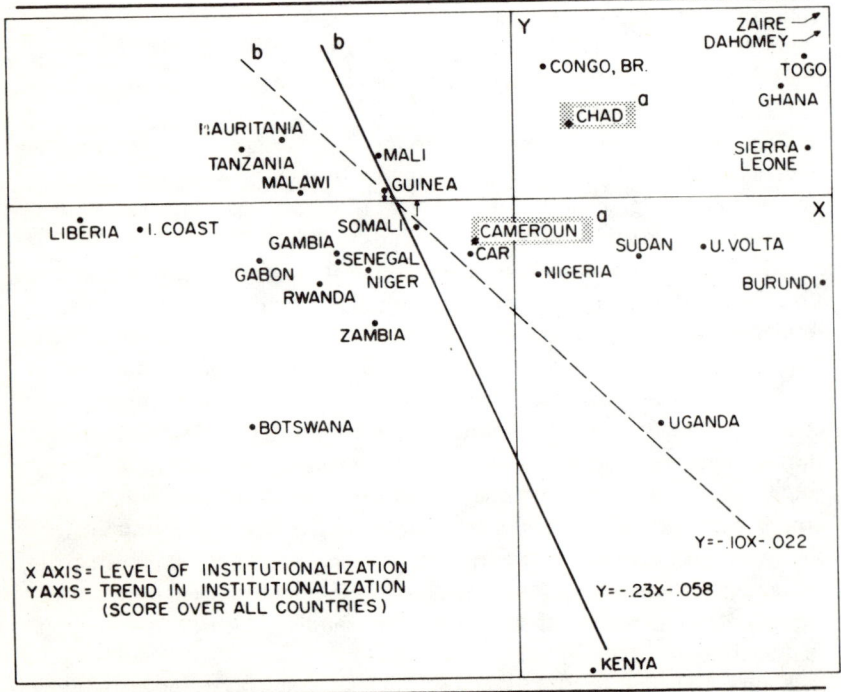

Figure 3: INSTITUTIONALIZATION IN THE DISCRIMINATION OF COUP AND NONCOUP COUNTRIES

Y = −.10X −.022 would satisfy as a discriminant. Third, and perhaps most important, our ability to discriminate clearly groups together all countries which have experienced a coup. That is, we can account successfully for all the coups that have occurred to date. Our only misclassifications are two countries for which we would predict a coup but in which one has not yet occurred. One could conjecture particularistic explanations for Cameroun and Chad (e.g., the presence of the French army in Chad), but the ability to perfectly discriminate countries which have experienced coups on the basis of level and process of party system institutionalization not only further supports the validity of the concept, but also demonstrates the relevance of the distinction between condition and process.

The analysis of trend has investigated regularities in the time series, but an additional question of interest is the existence of discontinuities. Here the concern is with abrupt, or step, changes in the level of institutionalization rather than a general rise or fall. But whether or not a series experiences these abrupt jumps brings us close to more theoretical questions of causation—what accounts for sharp changes in a system's level of institutionalization? This is not to deny underlying causes of trend but these tend to be more subtle influences than those accounting for discontinuities. The next section focuses on possible discontinuities in political institutionalization associated with one important event, national political independence.

DISCONTINUITIES OF POLITICAL INDEPENDENCE

Independence, or the end of colonial rule, is one of the most obvious events which might cause abrupt changes in a party system's institutionalization. Political parties under colonial rule have only minor opportunities to control authoritative positions, but with the advent of independence the political system falls under the influence of indigenous parties. In other words, pre- and postindependence constitute two very distinct periods for African party systems. The actual direction of effect that independence could have, however, is not so clear. On the one hand, one could hypothesize that independence would have an adverse effect on institutionalization. It has been argued that the end of colonial rule brings a dissolution of unity which is highly conducive to social conflict among ethnic or religious groups and in-fighting among political elites (Willner and Willner, 1965; Wriggins, 1961). The latter condition is held to be detrimental to party system institutionalization in failing to provide a stable environment for institutional development and in encouraging a focus on the ends of power and control at the expense of recruitment and political process. Similarly, the dispersion of resources after independence has been seen as detrimental to institutionalization. During the colonial period those few members of the indigenous population that had acquired "modern" political skills tended to be concentrated in the party system. But the emergence of new political roles (e.g., in the bureaucracy) siphoned off personnel from the party system resulting in institutional weakness (Foltz, 1963; Wallerstein, 1966). In Huntington's (1965: 425) words, "(a) marked dispersion of resources means a decline in the overall level of political institutionalization." In the opposite vein, it is plausible that colonial experience was the debilitating element, and that African countries are having some success in recovering from that experience by gradually building viable national political institutions. The fact of independence, and, hence, an ability to freely probe and experiment, may encourage institutionalization.

Whatever the specific effect, the advent of independence is a sufficiently extraordinary event to have a potential impact on party system institutionalization. In addition we can look at independence as a dividing line in the history of a party system and investigate the question of whether preindependence institutionalization has any effect on postindependence institutionalization. Several strategies are used to probe these questions relating to the impact of independence. First is a comparison of the levels of institutionalization before and after independence to investigate whether levels under colonial rule play some part in determining levels after independence; second is an examination of postindependence trends to discover whether the end of colonial rule is followed by significant processes of institutionalization; and finally an interrupted time series quasi-experimental design is employed to ascertain whether independence is followed by significant changes in level and slope.

LEVEL OF INSTITUTIONALIZATION:
PRE- AND POSTINDEPENDENCE

Considering the various effects that independence might have on institutionalization, it is hypothesized here that the general relationship between pre- and postindependence levels of institutionalization is one of positive feedback. If a party system is relatively institutionalized early in time, independence provides the opportunity for increasing institutionalization. On the other hand, if a party system is relatively uninstitutionalized, the new situations presented by independence are likely to increase the level of uninstitutionalization. In other words, the preindependence period is predicted to determine in large part positions after independence, with institutionalizaed and uninstitutionalized systems tending to diverge.

In order to test this hypothesis several subtests are required. First the correlation between the pre- and postindependence scores should be positive, and second it should be high. Third, in a regression analysis, the slope of the regression line should be greater than 1.00. That is, for every unit of institutionalization before independence, there would be more than one unit after independence. This third test reveals whether institutionalization is a self-reinforcing process.

Institutionalization scores were obtained for the pre- and postindependence periods by calculating the mean standard scores of the thirteen indicators separately for the two periods. The correlation between the two period scores is .63. Thus the relationship is positive and high enough to indicate that the preindependence years are an important factor in determining levels of institutionalization after independence. However, the relationship does not seem sufficiently strong to confirm the hypothesis. Clearly some party systems are moving in directions not predicted on the basis of institutionalization before independence, since preindependence scores account for only about 40% of the variation in postindependence levels of institutionalization. The slope of the regression line is .71 (the regression equation is $y = .71x - .004$), which clearly disconfirms the notion of positive feedback, and indicates that institutionalized systems tend to become relatively less so, while uninstitutionalized systems become relatively more institutionalized. Thus, rather than party systems diverging in their institutionalization, there appears to be a convergence toward the center.[17]

Because of the imperfect relationship between the two scores, a visual presentation helps to identify those cases that diverge from predicted positions and to indicate the adequacy of the relationship across ranges of the two variables. Figure 4 is the plot between the preindependence and postindependence scores. It should be noted first that the plot reveals that those countries which were concluded on the basis of Table 6 above to have experienced significant trends during the duration of their party systems do experience shifts in their mean level from pre- to postindependence in the direction indicated by those significant trends. Most obvious examples are Niger and Kenya, which have had institutionalizing trends and in Figure 4 are considerably more institutionalized after independence than before, and Dahomey and Mauritania, which have uninstitutionalizing trends and in Figure 4 are considerably less institutionalized after independence. Mali alone is problematic, for in spite of its significant uninstitutionalizing trend its static postindependence condition is seemingly slightly more institutionalized. Examination of the yearly scores for each of the indicators, however, leads me to conclude that this apparent shift in the level for the two periods is artifactual, and due primarily to a relatively large number of postindependence indicators with no yearly variance which inappropriately compensate for the highly uninstitutional scores on participation, legal single party, electoral discrimination, and arrests. The uninstitutionalizing trend presented in Table 6 is accepted, here, as the more accurate representation of temporal developments in Mali.

Inspection of Figure 4 reveals that with two exceptions—Congo Brazzaville and Lesotho—all systems that were relatively institutionalized in the preindependence period were also institutionalized after independence (i.e., are located in quadrant I). None of the party systems that were relatively institutionalized prior to independence deviate noticeably from the regression line except for Lesotho, which remains a significant deviant case. Congo Brazzaville was just slightly institutionalized before independence and slightly uninstitutionalized afterwards, but that could be interpreted as random fluctuation. Apart from Lesotho, then, the pattern seems clear that systems that became relatively institutionalized during the colonial period perpetuated that condition after independence.

The uninstitutionalized systems are obviously far less predictable and essentially fall into three groups. There are five that fall fairly close to the values predicted from the overall regression equation. This group, which will be labeled "predictables," includes Ghana, Sudan, Nigeria, Chad, and Cameroun (the last has become slightly institutionalized in what, again, might be called a random fluctuation). Six countries that were uninstitutionalized before independence have, or had, become considerably more institutionalized after independence. These are Sierra Leone, Upper Volta, Uganda, Kenya, Niger, and CAR, and will be called "decelerators" since their level of uninstitutionalization dropped markedly; all but Sierra Leone moved to a relatively institutionalized position. Finally there are four that were uninstitutionalized before independence but became considerably more uninstitutionalized later. Included in this group of "accelerators" (the level of uninstitutionalization increases sharply) are Zaire, Dahomey, Burundi, and Togo. Table 7 lists all of the party systems and provides a measure of deviation of actual postindependence scores from that predicted by the regression equation.

In seeking explanations for these three patterns among the uninstitutionalized preindependence party systems, one might suggest that different levels of uninstitutionalization could determine later patterns. Thus, it is hypothesized that uninstitutionalization is self-aggravating at higher levels, self-maintaining at moderate levels, and self-adjusting at lower levels. In terms of preindependence scores, accelerators are expected to have had the

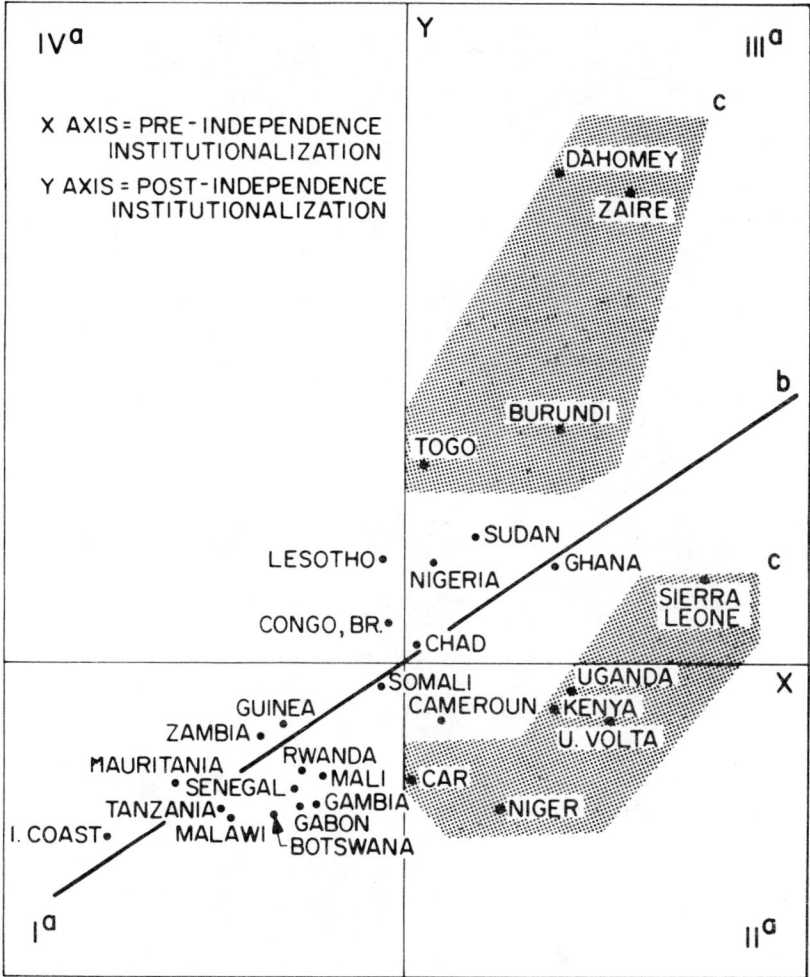

Figure 4: PLOT BETWEEN PRE- AND POSTINDEPENDENCE INSTITUTIONALIZATION SCORES

a. Quadrant I includes party systems relatively institutionalized pre- and postindependence. Quadrant II includes party systems relatively uninstitutionalized preindependence but institutionalized postindependence. Quadrant III includes party systems relatively uninstitutionalized pre- and postindependence. Quadrant IV includes party systems relatively institutionalized preindependence but uninstitutionalized postindependence.

b. The nearly diagonal line plots the best-fitting regression of postindependence scores on preindependence scores and is given by the equation $y = .71x - .004$.

TABLE 7
RESIDUALS OF PREDICTABLES, ACCELERATORS, DECELERATORS, AND PREINDEPENDENCE INSTITUTIONALIZED SYSTEMS

Group	Country	Residual
Predictable	Cameroun	−.25
Uninstitutionalized	Chad	.02
	Ghana	−.07
	Nigeria	.22
	Sudan	.22
Accelerators	Burundi	.40
	Zaire	.99
	Dahomey	1.17
	Togo	.57
Decelerators	CAR	−.38
	Kenya	−.50
	Niger	−.69
	Sierra Leone	−.43
	Uganda	−.45
	Upper Volta	−.66
Institutionalized	Botswana	−.17
	Congo, B	.16
	Gabon	−.22
	Gambia	−.26
	Guinea	.10
	Ivory Coast	.14
	Malawi	−.07
	Mali	−.18
	Mauritania	.17
	Rwanda	−.11
	Senegal	−.15
	Somali	−.01
	Tanzania	−.03
	Zambia	.11
	Lesotho	.37

highest levels of uninstitutionalization, predictables should have had moderate levels, and decelerators low levels. An analysis of variance on preindependence scores, however, revealed that there was no significant difference among the three groups in any direction. Table 8 presents the small and insignificant differences among the three groups in levels of preindependence institutionalization.

A second hypothesis is that the three groups differ in the consistency of their preindependence institutionalization, where consistency is indicated by variation across the set of separate indicators employed in this analysis. Thus some might be consistently uninstitutionalized, while others might exhibit low scores on some indicators and high scores on others. The latter pattern could be taken as indicative of system ambiguity, and later observations might reveal a shift in level of institutionalization as the system becomes more consistent. The particular hypothesis of interest is that both accelerators and decelerators (i.e., those that shift) are more inconsistent in levels of preindependence institutionalization than are the predictables. An acceptable measure of consistency is the standard deviation across indicators for each of the countries. This measure was employed in an analysis of variance for two groups (the shifters and predictables). The results, reported in Table 8, reveal that accelerators and decelerators are indeed significantly less consistent across indicators in the early period. Those sytems which were predicted well on the basis of their preindependence scores were relatively consistent in their uninstitutionalization, but both the accelerators and decelerators were inconsistent and, thus, their levels of institutionalization were more uncertain, facilitating a shift to more consistent positions.

Given inconsistent patterns, a legitimate question relates to what variables, if any, systematically contribute to the inconsistency found among the accelerators and decelerators. That is, in what ways are the accelerators and decelerators different? The question is posed in exploratory terms, since particular hypotheses are not apparent. An examination of the indicators used here revealed no systematic differences between the two groups (individual countries exhibited high and low scores on variables apparently randomly), with the exception of national orientation. That variable provides a perfect discrimination, such that no accelerator has a raw score on national orientation greater than 3.3, while no decelerator has a score less than 3.5. In short, uninstitutionalized systems that consisted of primarily nationally oriented parties at independence became relatively institutionalized, while systems of regionally or ethnically oriented parties became more uninstitutionalized. Significant differences also obtain when the predictables are included. Table 8 presents the differences among the three groups on national orientation, revealing the intermediate position of the predictables.

Preindependence levels of institutionalization determine in large part the status of the party system after independence. The linear relationship is most clear among the institutionalized systems. The postindependence levels of those systems that were consistently uninstitutionalized before independence were also predicted well. Ten party systems required more knowledge than simply preindependence level of institutionalization, however, to predict their later positions. These ten (four accelerators and six decelerators) were inconsistent in their institutionalization, scoring

TABLE 8
ANALYSES OF VARIANCE OF PREINDEPENDENCE UNINSTITUTIONALIZED PARTY SYSTEMS

	Predictables		Accelerators		Decelerators		F	df
	$\bar{X}$	sd	$\bar{X}$	sd	$\bar{X}$	sd		
Mean Preindependence Uninstitutionalization	.21	.18	.45	.29	.51	.33	1.73	2 12
sd of Preindependence Uninstitutionalization	.78	.10	$\bar{X}$ 1.10	sd .27			6.25[a]	1 13
National Orientation Standard Score[b]	.75	.54	1.43	.58	−.08	.84	5.01[a]	2 11

a. significant at or beyond .05 level
b. measured at independence election

high on some variables and low on others, and it was the national orientation of the party system that successfully discriminated (and hence possibly determined) the direction in which the party system would move in the postindependence period.

PROCESSES OF INSTITUTIONALIZATION IN THE POSTINDEPENDENCE PERIOD

Previous time series analyses revealed that only a minority of the 31 party systems exhibited significant processes of institutionalization for the period 1945-1970. It could be argued, however, that inclusion of preindependence years in that analysis masked real processes that might be occurring in some countries. The rationale for such an argument is that while we recognize the impact of preindependence experience on relative postindependence levels of institutionalization, the true unfolding, or development, of systems in one direction or another may require greater latitude than existed under colonial rule. Systems, perhaps, are "becoming" (not, are being) very different entities when they are without the formal constraints of colonialism. In that sense the occurrence of independence might be viewed as a "discontinuity" in the series marking a point at which different processes can and do occur. Since party systems were somewhat constrained under colonial rule perhaps the relevant question is that once freed of this constraint do party systems exhibit a significant process of institutionalization.

Investigation of postindependence [18] slopes reveals that more systems experience significant trends here than in the total time period in spite of fewer observations and, hence, greater standard errors of estimate.

[53]

Twenty-five of the 31 party systems have a sufficient number of years after independence on which to calculate a slope (six years is taken as the minimum here), and of these, twelve, or approximately 50%, exhibit slopes significantly different from zero. Table 9 gives the twelve party systems with significant postindependence trends.

The brevity of the period after independence makes it risky to place too much of a definitive interpretation on the postindependence trends. The fact that two countries (Chad and Mali) have a direction of trend for the postindependence period different from that for the total period could be due to the few years after independence which may not illuminate patterns that have and could emerge over a longer period of time. Hence, one might argue that in these two cases at least, the postindependence trend is spurious. By the same token, one ought to emphasize the problems that inclusion of the colonial years could pose, since, as indicated above, colonial rule might constrain normal party system developments and thus affect basic processes. It is quite possible that both trends are meaningful—that relative to the colonial period these countries were becoming less institutionalized but in the years since independence they are beginning (or began) to experience a new process of becoming more institutionalized once freed of colonial domination.

If we can assume that these postindependence trends are indeed meaningful, Table 9 reveals some interesting points. Only one party system (Kenya) experienced a significant institutionalizing trend in the total period, but in the postcolonial years half of the twelve significant slopes are in an institutionalizing direction. Although three of these systems (Mali, Somali, and Upper Volta) have been terminated by coups, it appears that they had begun to raise their relatively low levels of institutionalization, and the other three (Chad, Niger, and Senegal) continued to do so through 1970. Clearly very different processes are occurring in each of the countries but at least a few of the party systems have had some success in becoming relatively more institutionalized. Whatever the direction of "becoming," however, a larger number of countries do experience processes of institutionalization after independence than during the 1945-1970 period. While it may be dangerous to place too much value on the slopes in Table 9, the number of trends relatively significantly different from zero raises the possibility that, in terms of process, considerably more is going on in these party systems after the end of colonial rule.

In summary, a comparison of pre- and postindependence levels of institutionalization indicates that later levels depend in part on early levels, and an investigation of postindependence slopes possibly warrants the conclusion that independence permits greater latitude for processes of

TABLE 9
SIGNIFICANT TRENDS: POSTINDEPENDENCE PERIOD

Country	Postindependence	
	Slope[a]	F[b]
Chad	−.028	3.754
Dahomey	+.116	2.037
Ivory Coast	+.008	3.454
Mali	−.040	10.068
Mauritania	+.026	10.333
Niger	−.064	17.867
Rwanda	+.020	2.149
Senegal	−.012	6.525
Somali	−.038	2.905
Tanzania	+.012	2.054
Upper Volta	−.144	15.673
Zambia	+.075	2.930

a. Scored over all countries. Negative signs indicate an institutionalizing movement, positive signs an uninstitutionalizing movement.
b. See Table 6 for an explanation of the F-statistic.

institutionalization to occur. An interrupted time series quasi-experiment on the other hand, enables us to determine whether the occurrence of independence actually marks a significant discontinuity in the level and/or process of institutionalization. The quasi-experimental investigation of discontinuities is handled in detail elsewhere (Duvall and Welfling, 1973), where it is concluded that in many systems independence does have a real impact on either the condition or process of institutionalization.

INSTITUTIONALIZATION: THEORETICAL RELATIONSHIPS

After arriving at a conceptualization of institutionalization, this paper has reported a variety of attempts to measure that concept among 31 political party systems in black Africa. Institutionalization has been analyzed as both a condition and process for the period 1945-1970, and postindependence levels and trends of party system institutionalization have been investigated, especially as they relate to the preindependence and total time periods. Thus the research reported has been largely descriptive in its application of institutionalization measures to African party systems. Some of the previous sections, particularly those on the impact of independence and the relationship of institutionalization to the occurrence of coups, however, began to raise more theoretical questions, and it is in large part the theoretical relevance of the concept of institutionalization that stimulated this investigation into the concept and its measurement.

Perhaps the two variables most often associated with institutionalization are social mobilization and political strife. Various relationships have been postulated, though few empirical works have been reported in support of these conjectures. When social mobilization is viewed as increased political awareness on the part of mobilized publics (generally due to increased education, literacy, and media exposure), it is generally proposed to strain existing institutions. Huntington's (1965: 386) well-known argument states that: "Rapid increases in mobilization and participation, the principal aspects of modernization, undermine political institutions. Rapid modernization, in brief, produces not political development but political decay." On the other hand, it might be argued that increased awareness serves to counteract the problems of personnel diffusion at independence by creating new elites, thereby affording the party system or other political organizations a necessary resource base for institutionalization. Also, increased awareness might be thought to facilitate communication by fostering a more widespread acceptance of shared symbols and hence it could be hypothesized to promote institutionalization.

When social mobilization is viewed more as economic development some suggest that increased wealth means increased government capability (Stevenson, 1971) which we would expect to be conducive to political institutionalization, particularly of systems linking governments and publics, while others note how economic development raises expectations and demands which in turn strain political institutions (Olson, 1963).

Finally, though social mobilization is generally viewed as the causal variable, rates of mobilization are conceivably dependent upon levels of political institutionalization. In a comparative study of Bolivia's MNR and Cuba's PCC, Dominguez and Mitchell (1972) investigate institutionalization as it relates to mobilization (defined as political participation and structural change) and the toleration of dissent. The choice of political mobilization or dissent leads to changes in levels of institutionalization (lower and higher, respectively) but the latter, in turn, affects later courses of development. The authors suggest that increases in institutionalization are likely to lead to increases in dissent but also to a drop in political mobilization.

The second factor frequently related to institutionalization is civil strife. One position states that moderately stressful events in the environment of a system will stimulate adaptability and institutional strength on the part of the system. Huntington (1965: 395), for instance, has proposed that "fierce conflict or other serious challenges may transform organizations into institutions much more rapidly than under normal circumstances," and more recently Popper (1971) argues that internal war, if not too severe, can be a stimulant to political development. But again the opposite argument can be found that institutions develop best in secure, stable environments. Weiner (1965: 64) holds that processes of national integration will be stimulated by the learning of rules of social conduct and national disintegration by the breaking of those rules, and Foltz (1963) maintains that nation-building can occur best where elites, at least, feel secure. The relationship is not unidirectional, and, as with mobilization, strife can be seen as dependent upon institutionalization. Zolberg (1968b) suggests that causes of military coups and the pervasiveness of conflict in Africa lie in the low levels of political institutionalization, and the research reported above strongly supports the relationship between institutionalization and coups. Institutionalization seems relevant not only to elite forms of instability but also to more widespread disorder since one would expect the mobilization of mass publics to lead to some form of violence in the absence of institutional linkages with the government. Gurr's (1968) earlier work on civil strife, for instance, postulates institutionalization as an intervening variable between discontent and instability, and the Schneider (and Schneider, 1971) test of Huntington's proposition finds that political violence, at least in ten wealthy nations, is most likely to occur when social mobilization outruns the development of political institutions.

A third concept less frequently related to institutionalization is government performance. Hudson (1967) has conceptualized institutionalization as intervening between stress and government performance, such that high stress leads to poor performance only in the absence of adequate institutionalization. Sandstrom (1972) has begun to look at similar relationships in his work on Jamaica. In addition, performance has a probable effect on institutionalization to the degree that poor performance constitutes stress on the system (Hudson, 1967), and as such might be expected to have effects on institutionalization similar to those of social mobilization and political strife.

Another factor that seems potentially important in its relationship to institutionalization is social structural characteristics. Features such as social heterogeneity and social inequality constitute strains that are likely to influence the process and condition of institutionalization. Where a party system engages in the task of linking publics with government, and where publics themselves are highly diverse and often antagonistic, institutionalization is probably more difficult. Being forced to link groups in a multiplicity of directions can strain a system beyond any ability to adapt to the cross pressures and stabilize interactions. This is not to say that processes of institutionalization are impossible where cleavages are severe, but that, particularly in new states, such strains render political institutionalization much more difficult.

The possible theoretical relationships of institutionalization are numerous, but many of the proposed relationships are actually contradictory, particularly those concerning its causes. Most of these contradictory hypotheses boil down to a disagreement whether insitutionalization is promoted more by a stable environment or a threatening, unstable, stressful, one. Do mobilization, strife, poor governmental performance, and structural strains constitute stresses that serve to stimulate institutional development or, in Huntington's terms, do they undermine institutions and produce decay? On the other hand, does effective institutionalization promote a stable environment by reducing strife, slowing mobilization, improving government performance, and reducing structural strains?

Since we lack systematic cross-national research no one is yet in a position to conclude definitively what are the relationships among these concepts. The author, however, has begun to test some of the relationships suggested here through hypothesis-testing and parameter-estimating research. The thrust of these efforts has been to demonstrate with some degree of adequacy that strife and institutionalization are interrelated, with institutionalization operating against strife, and strife having a complex relationship with institutionalization depending on the form of strife and prior level of institutionalization. In two separate analyses there is no evidence that mobilization promotes institutionalization but there is some evidence that in black Africa institutionalization may slow mobilization. These research efforts converge in suggesting that in the African context political institutionalization seems to act to create a more stable environment (by reducing conflict and slowing mobilization), and that institutionalization itself is in part a function of environmental stress (Duvall and Welfling, 1973; Welfling and Duvall, 1973). The author has not investigated government performance or structural strain, but based on results obtained from an investigation of mobilization and strife, it is conjectured that institutionalization would improve performance and reduce strain (i.e, stabilize the environment), while poor performance and structural stress could serve to stimulate institutional development.

Political institutionalization is an important concept in comparative politics, but few have begun to systematically probe its various causes and effects. The little cross-national work that has been done has produced to date more contradictions than answers, so the need for further investigations into the theoretical relationships of institutionalization in many contexts is readily apparent. Appropriate empirical tests, however, require a basis in clear conceptualization of relevant variables and their precise measurement. For that reason the primary emphases of this paper have been on attempting to adequately conceptualize and measure institutionalization although some attention has been given to its theoretical relationship investigated in work to date.

NOTES

1. For English translations of Weber's political sociology, see *From Max Weber: Essays in Sociology* (1947a), *The Theory of Social and Economic Organizations* (1947b), and *Max Weber on Law in Economy and Society* (1954). Weber relates political institutions to their historical contexts in *The Religion of China* (1951) and *The Religion of India* (1958). Excerpts from various translations can be found in Eisenstadt (1968); and Bendix (1962) is a helpful discussion of Weber's sociology.

2. Keohane (1969) comes very close to this perspective although his dimensions differ from the ones developed here.

3. The author is particularly grateful to comments by Kenneth Janda and Jorge Dominguez for a clarification of this point.

4. The 31 countries are: Botswana, Burundi, Cameroun, Central African Republic, Chad, Congo (Brazzaville), Dahomey, Gabon, Gambia, Ghana, Guinea, Ivory Coast, Kenya, Lesotho, Liberia, Malawi, Mali, Mauritania, Niger, Nigeria, Rwanda, Senegal, Sierra Leone, Somali, Sudan, Tanzania, Togo, Uganda, Upper Volta, Zaire, and Zambia.

5. A fuller discussion of both the rationale and measurement of indicators appears in Welfling (1971: ch. 4).

6. Since the distribution of this variable is highly skewed because of a preponderance of zero values, the square root of the percentage of seats won by independents was taken. The author has reservations about arbitrary transformations of variables but accepted the procedure in this case because the dimension of boundary was indicated only by this one variable.

7. Measures of legislative instability developed by Janda (1970) and Rae (1967) were rejected since they are affected by size of party (the smaller the party, the larger the instability), number of parties, and/or, most strangely, number of legislative seats.

8. The indicators splits, mergers, and name changes are adopted from Janda's (1970) measures of party institutionalization, although specific scoring procedures differ.

9. If a party held 10% of the seats, the event receives a score of .10. When the party never has held legislative seats, the event receives a score of .005, so that it is weighted less than a party with 1% of the seats, but still is scored.

10. Preprocessing the data revealed that name changes scored as raw number of events intercorrelated better with the other variables than the weighted score. The weighted score does not take into consideration the magnitude of the name change (Janda, 1970), and this factor is probably as important as the size of the party.

Possible distortions produced by this scoring procedure led to the use of simple number of name-changing events rather than the weighted score.

11. Valenzuela (1972) investigates the scope of the Chilean party system and employs MacRae's index of multiparty competition. This approach is not followed here, however, since it is felt that scope of party competition is not equivalent to scope of the party system, and from the practical side, since adequate electoral statistics are not available across all African countries to support such measures.

12. This difficulty has been raised in comments by Jorge Dominguez. The author would argue that certain indicators do not reflect primarily stability, but accepts Dominguez's suggestion that the indexing procedure of weighting equally all variables overweights stability, since there are more indicators of stability than of the other characteristics.

13. National Orientation was scored at only one time point—the independence election—because of a lack of documentation. Also recall that the scoring of the adaptability indicators does not begin until self-rule or independence. The scoring of indicators was done as archival research. A great variety of sources were searched varying with the country in question. Utilized for all countries were *Africa Diary; Africa Report; Africa Research Bulletin;* Reuters, *The New Africans: A Guide to the Contemporary History of Emergent Africa and Its Leaders* (New York: G. P. Putnam's Sons, 1967); and Ronald Segal, *Political Africa: A Who's Who of Personalities and Parties* (London: Stevens and Sons, 1961). In addition hundreds of country-specific works were examined. Data from Northwestern's National Integration Project (Morrison et al., 1972) were employed for electoral participation.

14. Note that Mali and Uganda have had coups since the publication of Zolberg's statement.

15. Lesotho is omitted from the validation since events surrounding chief Jonathon's illegal seizure of power were coded, building in a relationship between institutionalization scores and the nonmilitary coup.

16. Employing slopes scored by country results in a similar pattern. Cameroun falls below the line with noncoup countries, but Mali becomes a deviant falling below the line. Chad remains a deviant among the coup countries.

17. At least part of the convergence effect from pre to post is due to a statistical artifact in scoring the concept of institutionalization. All of the variables postindependence exhibit more positively skewed distributions than preindependence, except for arrests and banishments. Skewed distributions result in relatively large standard deviations, hence fewer cases can obtain large (in terms of absolute values) standard scores. The more highly skewed distributions, however, indicate that in fact more countries have zero values (or highly institutionalized raw scores) on many of the variables. That is, in raw score terms more countries are tending to become more institutionalized. The scoring technique employing standard scores is based on countries relative to one another so that countries appear to become less institutionalized after independence. Since analysis is based on systems relative to other systems, no analytic harm results from the scoring technique.

18. The postindependence period begins with self-rule for some countries and independence for others, depending on which event enabled indigenous political personnel to feel independent or relatively unconstrained in comparison to prior experience. In general, self-rule was taken as the most significant event for French and Belgian colonies, although Belgian colonies had either no period of self-rule or a very brief one, and independence the significant event for British colonies. For a further explanation see Duvall and Welfling (1973: 397-398).

REFERENCES

ALMOND, G. and G. B. POWELL (1966) Comparative Politics: A Developmental Approach. Boston: Little, Brown.
ASHBY, W. R. (1960) Design for a Brain. New York: John Wiley.
BENDIX, R. (1962) Max Weber: An Intellectual Portrait. Garden City, N.Y.: Doubleday Anchor.
BENJAMIN, R. and K. ORI (1970) "Some aspects of political party institutionalization in Japan." Tokyo: Sophia University Institute of International Relations for Advanced Studies on Peace and Development in Asia, Series A-1.
BENJAMIN, R. and T. PEDELISKI (1969) "The Minnesota public defender system and the criminal law process: a comparative study of behavior at the judicial district level." Law and Society Rev. 4 (November): 279-320.
BIENEN, H. (1970) "The ruling party in the African one-party state: TANU in Tanzania," pp. 68-83 in M. E. Doro and N. M. Stultz (eds.) Governing Black Africa. Englewood Cliffs, N.J.: Prentice-Hall.
BLAU, P. (1964) Exchange and Power in Social Life. New York: John Wiley.
BLUMER, H. (1962) "Society as symbolic interaction," pp. 179-192 in A. Rose (ed.) Human Behavior and Social Processes. Boston: Houghton Mifflin.
BRASS, P. (1969) "Political participation, institutionalization, and stability in India." Government and Opposition 4 (Winter): 23-53.
BUCKLEY, W. (1967) Sociology and Modern Systems Theory. Englewood Cliffs, N.J.: Prentice-Hall.
CAMPBELL, D. (1969) "Definitional versus multiple operationism." Et Al 2 (Summer): 14-17.
--- (1963) "From description to experimentation: interpreting trends as quasi-experiments," pp. 212-244 in C. Harris (ed.) Problems in Measuring Change. Madison: Univ. of Wisconsin Press.
CHAMBERS, W. (1966) "Parties and nation-building in America," pp. 79-106 in J. La Palombara and M. Weiner (eds.) Political Parties and Political Development. Princeton: Princeton Univ. Press.
COLEMAN, J. S. (1966) "Collective decisions." Soc. Inquiry 34: 166-181.
--- and C. ROSBERG (1964) Political Parties and National Integration in Tropical Africa. Berkeley: Univ. of California Press.
DEUTSCH, K. (1963) "Shifts in the balance of communication flows," pp. 727-739 in N. Polsby et al. (eds.) Politics and Social Life. Boston: Houghton Mifflin.
DOMINGUEZ, J. and C. MITCHELL (1972) "The roads not taken: institutionalization and political parties in Cuba and Bolivia." Presented at the American Political Science Association Convention, Washington, D.C., September.
DOUGLAS, W. A. (1963) "The role of political parties in the modernization process." Korean Q. 5 (Autumn): 37-42.
DUVALL, R. and M. WELFLING (1973) "Determinants of political institutionalization in black Africa: a quasi-experimental analysis." Compar. Pol. Studies (January): 387-417.
EISENSTADT, S. N. [ed.] (1968) Max Weber: on Charisma and Institution Building. Chicago: Univ. of Chicago Press.
--- (1966) Modernization: Protest and Change. Englewood Cliffs, N.J.: Prentice-Hall.

--- (1965) Essays on Comparative Institutions. New York: John Wiley.
--- (1964) "Breakdowns of modernization." Econ. Development and Cultural Change 12 (July): 345-367.
--- (1962) "Initial institutional patterns of political modernization." Civilization (Brussels) 12, 4: 461-472; (1963): 15-26.
--- (1957) "Sociological aspects of political development in underdeveloped countries." Econ. Development and Cultural Change 4: 289-307.
EMERSON, R. (1966) "Parties and national integration in Africa," pp. 267-301 in J. La Palombara and M. Weiner (eds.) Political Parties and Political Development. Princeton: Princeton Univ. Press.
FOLTZ, W. J. (1963) "Building the newest nations: short-run strategies and long-run problems," pp. 117-131 in K. Deutsch and W. J. Foltz (eds.) Nation-Building. New York: Atherton.
GOODE, W. (1960) "A theory of role strain." Amer. Soc. Rev. 25: 483-496.
GURR, T. (1968) "A causal model of civil strife: a comparative analysis using new indices." Amer. Pol. Sci. Rev. 62 (December): 1104-1124.
HALPERN, M. (1965) "The rate and costs of political development." Annals 358 (March): 20-28.
HOLTZMAN, W. (1963) "Statistical models for the study of change in the single case," pp. 199-212 in C. Harris (ed.) Problems in Measuring Change. Madison: Univ. of Wisconsin Press.
HOMANS, G. (1961) Social Behavior: Its Elementary Forms. London: Harcourt, Brace.
HOPKINS, R. (1970) "The role of the M. P. in Tanzania." Amer. Pol. Sci. Rev. 64 (September): 754-771.
--- (1969) "Political roles and political institutionalization." Presented at the American Political Science Association Convention. New York, September.
HUDSON, M. (1967) "Some quantitative indicators for explaining and evaluating national political performance." Presented at the American Political Science Association Convention. Chicago, September.
HUNTINGTON, S. P. (1968) Political Order in Changing Societies. New Haven: Yale Univ. Press.
--- (1966) "The political modernization of traditional monarchies." Daedelus: 763-787.
--- (1965) "Political development and political decay." World Politics 17 (April): 386-430.
JANDA, K. (1971) "A technique for assessing the conceptual equivalence of institutional variables across and within culture areas." Presented at the American Political Science Association Convention. Chicago, September.
--- (1970) "A conceptual framework for the comparative analysis of political parties." Sage Professional Papers in Comparative Politics 01-002. Beverly Hills: Sage Pubns.
--- (1969) "The international comparative political parties project." Presented at the American Political Science Association Convention, New York, September.
KEOHANE, R. (1969) "Institutionalization in the United Nations General Assembly." Internat. Organization 23 (Autumn): 859-896.
KESSELMAN, M. (1969) "Over institutionalization and political constraint." Presented at the American Political Science Association Convention, New York, September.

LA PALOMBARA, J. (1969) "Political power and political development." Yale Law Rev. 78 (June): 1253-1275.
LEWIS, W. A. (1965) Politics in West Africa. New York: Oxford Univ. Press.
MILLER, J. G. (1965) "Living systems: basic concepts; structure and process; cross-level hypotheses." Behav. Sci. 10: 337-411.
MILLER, N. (1970) "The rural African party: political participation in Tanzania." Amer. Pol. Sci. Rev. 64 (June): 548-571.
MITCHELL, W. (1967) Sociological Analysis and Politics: The Theories of Talcott Parsons. Englewood Cliffs, N.J.: Prentice-Hall.
MORRISON, D., R. MITCHELL, J. PADEN, and H. M. STEVENSON (1972) Black Africa: A Handbook. New York: Free Press.
OLSON, M. (1963) "Rapid growth as a destablizing force." J. of Econ. History 23 (December): 529-552.
PARSONS, T. (1961) "Order and community in the international system," pp. 120-129 in J. Rosenau (ed.) International Politics and Foreign Policy. New York: Free Press.
--- (1956) "A sociological approach to the theory of organizations." Admin. Sci. Q. 1 (July): 63-85, and 2 (September): 225-239.
--- (1951a) The Social System. New York: Free Press.
--- (1951b) Toward a General Theory of Action. Cambridge: Harvard Univ. Press.
--- (1949) Essays in Sociological Theory. New York: Free Press.
POLSBY, N. (1968) "The institutionalization of the U.S. House of Representatives." Amer. Pol. Sci. Rev. 62 (March): 144-168.
POPPER, F. (1971) "Internal war as a stimulant to political development." Compar. Pol. Studies 3 (January): 413-423.
PUTNAM, R. (1967) "Towards explaining military interventions in Latin American politics." World Politics 19 (October): 83-110.
PYE, L. (1965) "The concept of political development." Annals 358 (March): 1-13.
RAE, D. (1967) The Political Consequences of Electoral Laws. New Haven: Yale Univ. Press.
ROTBERG, R. (1966) "Modern African studies: problems and prospects." World Politics 18: 567-569.
RUSTOW, D. (1969) "The organization triumphs over its function." J. of Internat. Affairs 12, 1: 119-132.
SANDSTROM, H. M. (1972) "Black power and political change in Jamaica." Presented at the American Political Science Association Convention, Washington, D.C., September.
SCHNEIDER, P. and A. SCHNEIDER (1971) "Social mobilization, political institutions, and political violence: a cross-national analysis." Compar. Pol. Studies 4 (April): 69-90.
SELZNICK, P. (1957) Leadership in Administration. Evanston, Ill.: Row, Peterson.
SILVERT, K. (1965) "Parties and masses." Annals 358 (March): 101-108.
STEVENSON, H. M. (1971) "Conflict and instability in Africa." Ph.D. dissertation. Evanston, Ill.: Northwestern University.
SWEEN, J. and D. T. CAMPBELL (1965) "The interrupted time series as quasi-experiment: three tests of significance." Evanston, Ill.: Northwestern University Department of Psychology. (unpublished)
TAYLOR, M. and V. M. HERMAN (1971) "Party systems and government stability." Amer. Pol. Sci. Rev. 65 (March): 28-37.

VALENZUELA, A. (1972) "The scope of the Chilean party system." Compar. Politics 4 (January): 179-199.
VON VORYS, K. (1965) "Toward a concept of political development." Annals 358 (March): 14-19.
WALLERSTEIN, I. (1966) "The decline of the party in single-party African states," pp. 201-214 in J. La Palombara and M. Weiner (eds.) Political Parties and Political Development. Princeton: Princeton Univ. Press.
––– (1960) "Ethnicity and national integration in West Africa." Cahiers d'Etudes Africains 3 (October): 129-138.
WEBER, M. (1958) The Religion of India. New York: Free Press.
––– (1951) The Religion of China. New York: Free Press.
––– (1947a) From Max Weber: Essays in Sociology. New York: Oxford Univ. Press.
––– (1947b) The Theory of Social and Economic Organization. New York: Oxford Univ. Press.
WEINER, M. (1967) Party Building in a New Nation: The India National Congress. Chicago: Univ. of Chicago Press.
––– (1965) "Political integration and political development." Annals 358 (March): 52-64.
WELFLING, M. (1971) "Political institutionalization: the development of a concept and its empirical application to African party systems." Ph.D. dissertation. Evanston, Ill.: Northwestern University.
––– and R. DUVALL (1973) "Social mobilization, political institutionalization, and conflict in black Africa: a simple dynamic model." J. of Conflict Resolution 17 (December).
WILLNER, A. R. and D. WILLNER (1965) "The rise and role of charismatic leaders." Annals 358 (March): 77-88.
WRIGGINS, H. (1961) "Impediments to unity in new nations: the case of Ceylon." Amer. Pol. Sci. Rev. 55 (June): 313-320.
YEAGER, R. (1972) "Institutional synthesis and decay in micropolitical systems: a dialectical paradigm and East African example." Presented at the American Political Science Association Convention, Washington, D.C., September.
ZARTMAN, W. (1964) Destiny of Dynasty: The Search for Institutions in Morocco's Developing Society. Columbia: Univ. of South Carolina Press.
ZOLBERG, A. (1968a) "Military interventions in the new states of tropical Africa," pp. 71-98 in H. Bienen (ed.) The Military Intervenes. New York: Russell Sage.
––– (1968b) "The structure of political conflict in the new states of tropical Africa." Amer. Pol. Sci. Rev. 62 (September): 70-87.
––– (1964) One-Party Government in the Ivory Coast. Princeton: Princeton Univ. Press.
––– (1963) "Mass parties and national integration: the case of the Ivory Coast." J. of Politics 15 (February): 36-48.

MARY B. WELFLING has been Assistant Professor of Political Science at Virginia Polytechnic Institute and State University since receiving her Ph.D. from Northwestern University in 1971. Her articles will be found in Comparative Political Studies, Journal of Conflict Resolution, *and in collections of papers on social science methodology and African politics. She is currently investigating models of conflict in Africa.*

A Better Way of Getting New Information

Research, survey and policy studies that say what needs to be said—no more, no less.

The Sage Papers Program

Five regularly-issued original paperback series that bring, at an unusually low cost, the timely writings and findings of the international scholarly community. Since the material is updated on a continuing basis, each series rapidly becomes a unique repository of vital information.

Authoritative, and frequently seminal, works that NEED to be available

- To scholars and practitioners
- In university and institutional libraries
- In departmental collections
- For classroom adoption

Sage Professional Papers
COMPARATIVE POLITICS SERIES
INTERNATIONAL STUDIES SERIES
ADMINISTRATIVE AND POLICY STUDIES SERIES
AMERICAN POLITICS SERIES

Sage Policy Papers
THE WASHINGTON PAPERS

The Publishers of Professional Social Science
Beverly Hills • London

Sage Professional Papers in **Comparative Politics**

Editors: **Harry Eckstein,** *Princeton University,* **Ted Robert Gurr,** *Northwestern University,* and **Aristide R. Zolberg,** *University of Chicago.*

VOLUME 1 (1970)

01-001 **J.Z. Namenwirth & H. D. Lasswell,** The changing language of American values: a computer study of selected party platforms $2.50/£1.05

01-002 **K. Janda,** A conceptual framework for the comparative analysis of political parties $1.90/£.80

01-003 **K. Thompson,** Cross-national voting behavior research $1.50/£.60

01-004 **W. B. Quandt,** The comparative study of political elites $2.00/£.85

01-005 **M. C. Hudson,** Conditions of political violence and instability $1.90/£.80

01-006 **E. Ozbudun,** Party cohesion in western democracies $3.00/£1.30

01-007 **J. R. Nellis,** A model of developmental ideology in Africa $1.40/£.55

01-008 **A. Kornberg, et al.,** Semi-careers in political organizations $1.40/£.55

01-009 **F. I. Greenstein & S. Tarrow,** Political orientations of children $2.90/£1.25

01-010 **F. W. Riggs,** Administrative reform and political responsiveness: a theory of dynamic balance $1.50/£.60

01-011 **R. H. Donaldson & D. J. Waller,** Stasis and change in revolutionary elites: a comparative analysis of the 1956 Central Party Committees in China and the USSR $1.90/£.80

01-012 **R. A. Pride,** Origins of democracy: a cross-national study of mobilization, party systems and democratic stability $2.90/£1.25

VOLUME II (1971)

01-013 **S. Verba, et al.,** The modes of democratic participation $2.80/£1.20

01-014 **W. R. Schonfeld,** Youth and authority in France $2.80/£1.20

01-015 **S. J. Bodenheimer,** The ideology of developmentalism $2.40/£1.00

01-016 **L. Sigelman,** Modernization and the political system $2.50/£1.05

01-017 **H. Eckstein,** The evaluation of political performance: problems and dimensions $2.90/£1.25

01-018 **T. Gurr & M. McLelland,** Political performance: a twelve nation study $2.90/£1.25

01-019 **R. F. Moy,** A computer simulation of democratic political development $2.70/£1.15

01-020 **T. Nardin,** Violence and the state $2.70/£1.15

01-021 **W. Ilchman,** Comparative public administration and "conventional wisdom" $2.40/£1.00

01-022 **G. Bertsch,** Nation-building in Yugoslavia $2.25/£.95

01-023 **R. J. Willey,** Democracy in West German trade unions $2.40/£1.00

01-024 **R. Rogowski & L. Wasserspring,** Does political development exist? Corporatism in old and new societies $2.40/£1.00

VOLUME III (1972)

01-025 **W. T. Daly,** The revolutionary $2.10/£.90

01-026 **C. Stone,** Stratification and political change in Trinidad and Jamaica $2.10/£.90

01-027 **Z. Y. Gitelman,** The diffusion of political innovation: from Eastern Europe to the Soviet Union $2.50/£1.05

01-028 **D. P. Conradt,** The West German party system $2.40/£1.00

01-029 **J. R. Scarritt,** Political development and culture change theory [Africa] $2.50/£1.05

01-030 **M. D. Hayes,** Policy outputs in the Brazilian states $2.25/£.95

01-031 **B. Stallings,** Economic dependency in Africa and Latin America $2.50/£1.05

01-032 **J. T. Campos & J. F. McCamant,** Cleavage shift in Colombia: analysis of the 1970 elections $2.90/£1.25

01-033 **G. Field & J. Higley,** Elites in developed societies [Norway] $2.25/£.95

01-034 **J. S. Szyliowicz,** A political analysis of student activism [Turkey] $2.80/£1.20

01-035 **E. C. Hargrove,** Professional roles in society and government [England] $2.90/£1.25

01-036 **A. J. Sofranko & R. J. Bealer,** Unbalanced modernization and domestic instability $2.90/£1.25

VOLUME IV (1973)

01-037 **W. A. Cornelius,** Political learning among the migrant poor $2.90/£1.25

01-038 **J. W. White,** Political implications of cityward migration [Japan] $2.50/£1.05

01-039 **R. B. Stauffer,** Nation-building in a global economy: the role of the multi-national corporation $2.25/£.95

01-040 **A. Martin,** The politics of economic policy in the U.S. $2.50/£1.05

Forthcoming, summer/fall 1973

01-041 **M. B. Welfling,** Political Institutionalization [African party systems] $2.70*/£1.15

01-042 **B. Ames,** Rhetoric and reality in a militarized regime [Brazil] $2.40*/£1.00

01-043 **E. C. Browne,** Coalition theories $2.90*/£1.25

01-044 **M. Barrera,** Information and ideology: a study of Arturo Frondizi $2.40*/£1.00

*denotes tentative price

Papers 01-045 through 01-048 to be announced.

Sage Professional Papers

Editor: **Vincent Davis** and Maur...

VOLUME I (1972)

02-001	**E. E. Azar**, et al., Inte... events interaction ana... $2.80/£1.20
02-002	**J. H. Sigler**, et al., Ap... events data analysis
02-003	**J. C. Burt**, Decision n... the world population $2.25/£.95
02-004	**J. A. Caporaso**, Func... regional integration
02-005	**E. R. Wittkopf**, Weste... aid allocations $2.5
02-006	**T. L. Brewer**, Foreign... tions: American elite... variations in threat, t... surprise $2.50/£1.0
02-007	**W. F. Weiker**, Decent... ernment in moderniz... [Turkish provinces]
02-008	**F. A. Beer**, The politi... of alliances: benefits,... institutions in NATO
02-009	**C. Mesa-Lago**. The lal... employment, unempl... underemployment in... 1970 $2.70/£1.15
02-010	**P. M. Burgess & R. W**... cators of internationa... an assessment of ever... research $3.00/£1....
02-011	**W. Minter**, Imperial r... external dependency $2.70/£1.15

Sage Professional Papers i

Administrat

Editor: **H. George Frederickso**...

VOLUME I (1973)

03-001	**E. Ostrom, W. Baug**... **R. Parks, G. Whitak**... organization and th... police services $3....
03-002	**R. S. Ahlbrandt, Jr.**... protection services
03-003	**D. O. Porter** with D... **T. W. Porter**. The po... ing federal aid [loca... $3.00/£1.30
03-004	**J. P. Viteritti**, Police... pluralism in New Y... $2.70/£1.15
The 1973 summer/fall papers	
03-005	**R. L. Schott**, Profes... service: characteristi... tion of engineer fed...

ORDER FORM

name
_____

institution
_____

address
_____

city/state/zip
_____

Please enter subscription(s) to:

☐ Prof. Pprs. in Administrative & Policy Studies

☐ Prof. Pprs. in Comparative Politics

☐ Prof. Pprs. in American Politics

☐ Prof. Pprs. in International Studies

☐ The Washington Papers

Please send the individual papers whose numbers I have listed below:
_____
_____
_____

☐ Please invoice (INSTITUTIONS ONLY) quoting P.O. # _____ (shipping and handling additional on non-subscription orders)

☐ Payment enclosed (Sage pays shipping charges)

INSTITUTIONAL ORDERS FOR LESS THAN $10.00 AND *ALL* PERSONAL ORDERS *MUST BE PREPAID*. (California residents: please add 6% sales tax on non-subscription orders.)

MAIL TO:

 SAGE Publications, Inc. / P.O. Box 5024 Beverly Hills, California 90210

orders from the U.K., Europe, the Middle East and Africa should be sent to Sage Publications, Ltd, 44 Hatton Garden, London EC1N 8ER

A Sage Policy Papers Series

The Washington Papers

... intended to meet the need for authoritative, yet prompt, public appraisal of the major changes in world affairs. Commissioned and written under the auspices of the Center for Strategic and international Studies (CSIS), Georgetown University, Washington, D.C. and published for CSIS by SAGE Publications; Beverly Hills/London.

Series Editor: **Walter Laqueur**, *Director of the Institute of Contemporary History (London) and Chairman, CSIS, Research Council, Georgetown University*

Price Information: Individual papers in the series are available at $2.50/£1.00 each.

Save on subscriptions: Individuals and institutions can realize substantial savings by entering a subscription order (commencing with Volume I) at the prices given below.

	1 year†	2 year	3 year
Institutional	$20/£8.50	$39/£16.50	$57/£24.00
Individual	$12/£5.40	$23/£10.40	$33/£15.40

†*See note on frequency below*

Frequency: Volume 1 (September 1972 through December 1973) will include 12 papers published over a 16-month period. Beginning with Volume II (1974), Ten papers will be published each calendar year—and mailed to subscribers in groups of 3 or 4 throughout the year.

Specially commissioned to bring you authoritative evaluations of major events affecting (and affected by) current developments in U.S. foreign policy and world affairs. THE WASHINGTON PAPERS offer timely, provocative, in-depth analyses by leading authorities—who also suggest likely future developments and analyze the policy implications of recent trends.

VOLUME I (1972-73) — $2.50 each / £1.00

- WP-1 R. M. Burrell, The Persian Gulf
- WP-2 R. Scalapino, American-Japanese relations in a changing era
- WP-3 E. Luttwak, The strategic balance, 1972
- WP-4 C. Issawi, Oil, the Middle East and the world
- WP-5 W. Laqueur, Neo-isolationism and the world of the seventies
- WP-6 W. E. Griffith, Peking, Moscow and beyond
- WP-7 R. M. Burrell & A. J. Cottrell, Politics, oil and the western Mediterranean
- WP-8 P. Hassner, Europe in the age of negotiation
- WP-9 W. Joshua & W. F. Hahn, Nuclear politics: America, France and Britain

Forthcoming
- WP-10 T. A. Sumberg, Foreign aid as a moral obligation?
- WP-11 H. Block, Trade with the Soviet Union
- WP-12 R. Moss, Hijacking

Sage Professional Papers in **American Politics**

Editor: **Randall B. Ripley**, *Ohio State University.*

VOLUME I (1973)

- 04-001 S. S. Nagel, Comparing elected and appointed judicial systems $2.25/£1.95
- 04-002 J. Dennis, Political socialization research: a bibliography $2.40/£1.00
- 04-003 H. B. Asher, Freshman representatives and the learning of voting cues $2.50/£1.05
- 04-004 J. Fishel, Representation and responsiveness in Congress: "the class of eighty-nine," 1965-1970 $2.70/£1.15

Papers 04-005 through 04-012 to be announced

MAIL TO
SAGE Publications / P.O. Box 5024 / Beverly Hills, Calif. 90210
orders from the U.K., Europe, the Middle East and Africa should be sent to 44 Hatton Garden, London EC1N 8ER